ESCOFFIER'S
BASIC ELEMENTS OF
FINE COOKERY
Including Sauces and Garnishes

MOULDS

Easter Egg

Porcelain Cases

Pound Cake

Cassolet

Gratin

Dome

Ice Cream

Cutlet

Bombe

Terrine à Paté

Brioche

Tartlet — Croustade

Ornamental Border

Parfait

Madeleine

Charlotte

Salamander

Conical — Pyramid

Cocotte

Dariole — Baba Timbale

Petit Four

Star

Larding Needle

Spring-Form — Flawn-Ring

Tart

Savarin — Ring — Border

Courtesy Bazar Français, New York

ESCOFFIER'S
BASIC ELEMENTS
OF FINE COOKERY

Including Sauces and Garnishes

by A. ESCOFFIER

✦

CRESCENT BOOKS, INC.

New York

WEIGHTS AND MEASUREMENTS

1 quart	=	4 cups	=	64 tbsp.
1 pint	=	2 cups	=	32 tbsp.
$\frac{1}{2}$ pint	=	1 cup	=	16 tbsp.
$\frac{1}{3}$ pint	=	$\frac{2}{3}$ cup	=	10$\frac{2}{3}$ tbsp.
$\frac{1}{4}$ pint	=	$\frac{1}{2}$ cup	=	8 tbsp.
$\frac{1}{8}$ pint	=	$\frac{2}{5}$ cup	= app.	6$\frac{1}{4}$ tbsp.
1 tbsp.	=			3 tsp.

BUTTER, One pound	=	2 cups
FLOUR, One pound	=	4 cups
SUGAR, One pound	=	2$\frac{1}{4}$ cups
1 tbsp. CORNSTARCH	=	$\frac{1}{3}$ ounce
1 tbsp. FLOUR	=	$\frac{1}{4}$ ounce

© MCMXLI, by Crown Publishers, Inc.
Library of Congress Catalog Card Number: 66-22655

Printed in the U.S.A.

This edition published by Crescent Books, Inc.,
a division of Crown Publishers, Inc.
CDEFGH

PUBLISHERS' NOTE

Escoffier's Basic Elements of Fine Cooking, Including Sauces and Garnishes appeared in the American edition of the great French Master Chef's world famous *Guide Culinaire*. Everything in it is stated in American terms and according to American usage.

In the translation, the publishers have been careful to retain the precise sense of Escoffier's writing. Therefore, Escoffier's recipes for certain foreign foods that are not usually obtainable in the U. S. have been retained for the benefit of those who may desire them. In such cases the American equivalents of the foreign foods are stated.

Likewise, certain French cooking terms have been used throughout the book because they do not bear exact translation (for example, *poëling,* which means roasting with butter). They are fully explained, however, both in the recipes where they appear and in the Glossary.

Recipes 1 through 279 appear in the book in normal sequence. Recipes with other numbers are to be found in the Appendix.

The Index contains a listing for each recipe under its French as well as English title, together with page and recipe numbers.

Terms that are defined in the Glossary are printed in italics. When, in one recipe, M. Escoffier refers to another recipe, the number of that recipe is given in parentheses.

The discussions preceding each type of food are eminently interesting and informing and the publishers suggest that readers consult these discussions before proceeding to prepare any of the excellent dishes described.

CONTENTS

GLOSSARY

Abats, refers to such butcher's specialties as heads, hearts, liver, kidneys, giblets, etc.

Aiguilettes, these are simply the breasts of the fowl cut into very thin slices.

Ailerons (wings).

Amourettes, the spinal marrow of the calf.

Anglaise, to treat à la Anglaise, see No. 174. Or to cook à la Anglaise, means to cook plainly in water. Also a preparation of beaten eggs and seasoning and oil.

Aromatics, No. 174a, this term mainly pertains to seasonings and herbs, but in many cases the author has used it to indicate a vegetable garnish, such as carrots, onions, etc., as in the preparation of a *Poëlé,* see No. 250.

Attereaux, bits of meat cooked on small skewers.

Baba mould, see Drawing.

Bain-marie, a hot water bath used for cooking or for keeping warm various preparations. At times an ordinary double-boiler will serve the same purpose, if the recipe indicates small quantities.

Barquettes, these are simply boat-shaped pastry shells used for garnishing.

Bavarois, this is the Bavarian Cream.

Biscottes, these are a light kind of dry rusk.

Bisque, see No. 241.

Blanched, see No. 273.

Bombe mould, see Drawing.

Border mould, see Drawing.

Braising, see Nos. 247 and 248. The traditional French method of braising is apt to be confusing so it is best to consult the chapters on this subject, which explain in detail. For other types of braisings consult the index.

Brandade, see No. 127, a mixture of a sauce and shredded fish, usually salt cod.

Brioche mould, see Drawing.

Brochettes, means to stick small pieces of meat on a skewer and cook in this manner.

Brunoise fashion, to cut food into small dice.

Caramel Sugar or Stage, see No. 2344.

Casserole (En), see No. 250.

Cassolet Mould, see Drawing.

Cèpes, a kind of mushroom.

Charlotte Mould, see Drawing.

Chartreuse, see No. 1220.

Chiffonade, see No. 215.

Choux, a kind of cake made from pâte a Choux. (Cream Puff Paste).

Civet, this is jugged hare.

Cocotte Mould, see Drawing.

Court-Boullion, see page 64.

Croustade Mould, see Drawing.

Croutons, pieces of bread in various shapes and sizes, fried in butter. Aspic jelly croutons are used to garnish cold dishes or salads.

Cullis, see No. 240.

Cutlet Mould, see Drawing.

Dariole Mould, see Drawing.

Darne, see No. 270, this is simply a large slice or cut, usually of salmon or other large fish.

Dome Mould, see Drawing.

Duxelles, see page 94.

Egg Mould, see Drawing.

Émincé, this simply means that the food is cut into a fine mince.

Essence, see Nos. 13 and 2354. The word essence when applied to meats, vegetables, etc., means a concentrate of that particular product, but when indicated in a pastry or dessert recipe it means flavoring or extract.

Fecula, this is pure starch and is principally used for thickening. Cornstarch, flour, etc., may be used.

Feuilletés, these are little pastries made of puff pastry in oval, round, or other shapes, used for appetizers, soups, etc.

Fines Herbes, see No. 174a. Minced fine dry herbs. But if the recipe calls for a herb sauce, see No. 132.

Flawn-ring (Spring-form), see Drawing.

Flute, a long crisp French dinner roll used in soups.

Foie-Gras, fat goose liver which is sometimes used uncooked or cooked in the recipes. At other times it is the prepared pâté type which is called for.

Fondue, it is either a cheese preparation or a pulpy state to which vegetables like tomatoes, sorrel, etc., are reduced by cooking.

Forcemeat, see page 78 under stuffings and forcemeat.

Fricandeau, is a large larded slice of veal from off the rump, similar to the Wiener Schnitzel.

Fumet, see No. 11. This is a kind of concentrated essence extracted from fish, game, by slow cooking.

Galette, any food formed into the shape of a small cake or patty.

Garbures, this is nothing more than a thick vegetable soup or hodge-podge.

Gaufrette, a thin wafer used in dessert preparations and for garnishes.

Glaze, the author has used this term to indicate a method of procedure in the use of concentrated essence which gives a glossy covering, and it may differ according to the recipe in which it is used. Therefore it is important that the reader refer to the index, according to whether the recipe calls for meat, game, fish, etc.

Godiveau, see No. 198

Granité, is very much like a sherbet.

Gratin or Gratined, see Nos. 268 to 272 inclusive.

Gratin Dish or Mould, see Drawing.

Grenadin, are small slices of veal on the order of very small veal cutlets, prepared according to the given recipe.

Ice Cream Mould, see Drawing.

Jardinières, this is a vegetable soup or sauce, or a mode of garnishing with garden vegetables.

Julienne, means to cut a product into long matched-shaped sticks.

Lard, See Stud (Glossary).

Larding Needle, see Drawing.

Lenten, simply means cooking without meat.

Macédoine, this is a mixture of early season vegetables and/or fruit.

Madeleine Mould, see Drawing.

Maigre (lean), refers to any dish prepared in the Lenten style, meaning without meat.

Maintenon, see No. 226.

Manié (butter and flour), see No. 151.

Manque Mould, a fancy mould.

Marinade or Marinate, see pages 64 to 69, inclusive. Means the liquid and to soak or steep the product in a prepared sauce or liquid prior to cooking it.

Matelotes, see Nos. 1037–38.

Matignon, see No. 227.

Mignonette, this is a peeled finest quality peppercorn.

Milt, this is another name for fish roe.

Minion Fillets, when used in a recipe for poultry or fowl of any kind, game birds, etc., it pertains to that part of the breast meat that lies right next to the *Suprême,* the largest muscles in the poultry breast. In the four footed animals it is the tenderloin.

Mirepoix, see No. 228.

Mise-en-Place, a general name given to those elementary preparations which are constantly resorted to during the various stages of most culinary operations.

Mousses, a class of light, hot or cold preparations of fish, meat, poultry, etc., and sweets, formed in large moulds large enough to serve a number of persons.

Mousselines, this is the same preparation as the *Mousse,* except that it is made in individual moulds.

Noisettes, these are small kernels of meat like the center part of a rib chop. It is really a part of the tenderloin like the tournedos of beef.

Oxalis Roots, this is a Mexican vegetable with a leaf similar to sorrel. It is a tuberous plant and the roots are very much like the ordinary potato and the latter or the Jerusalem artichoke may be used to replace it.

Orgeat, this is a preparation from orange-flower water, sugar and almonds, made into a thick syrup.

Ornamented Border Mould, see Drawing.

Palmettes, palm-shaped pieces of puff paste used in decorating.

Panada, see No. 189 under stuffings and forcemeat.

Panés à la Anglaise, see No. 174. Means covered with bread-crumbs.

Pannequets, similar to pancakes.

Papillote means wrapping the preparation in vegetable parchment and cooking it that way in the oven.

Parfait Mould, see Drawing.

Pâte à Choux is the kind of paste used for ordinary cream puff shells.

Pauppiette, any preparation rolled into a roulade or scroll and cooked in a like manner.

Paysanne, to cut the food or product into triangles.

Petit Four Mould, see Drawing.

Pig's Caul, this is the investing membrane, with fatty veins, which covers the intestinal organs of the pig. It is used by butchers in the preparation of certain cuts of meat for cooking and is therefore difficult to procure except at slaughter houses.

Pluches, principally applied to Chervil, but they may be the serrated portions of any leaves, such as tarragon, mint, etc.

Poach, see No. 249. This term means cooking very slowly in small amounts of water at the lowest temperature. It is best to refer to the description when in doubt about the method used.

Poêlé, see No. 250. A method of cooking used in France which should be called simply "butter roasting." It applies not only to meats, but to eggs, etc.

Porcelain Cases, see Drawing.

Pound Cake Mould, see Drawing.

Printanier, this usually means a garnish or filling of early spring vegetables cut into various shapes. It may also apply to preparations comprising the same.

Profiterolles, see No. 218.

Provençale, see No. 235. This is a special blend of Bechamel, with eggs and seasoning, used for stuffing foods, particularly cutlets a la Provençale.

Purée, a purée is any food that is strained through a sieve, so that it forms a complete mass. The consistency of the product referred to in the recipe and its use governs this. Purée not only applies to soups or sauces, etc., but to fruits, vegetables, meats, etc. In other words, any food.

Pyramid Mould, see Drawing.

Quenelle, see No. 205. These are forcemeat balls used for garnishing soup, etc.

Râble, the back or saddle of a hare.

Raspings, see No. 178. Simply the grated crusts of bread, etc., used for gratins, a l'Anglaise, etc.

Ravioli, an Italian form of filled paste, which is boiled and covered with a sauce.

Richelieu Mould, a deep fluted mould.

Risotta or Rizotto, is an Italian national dish. Rice, cooked with saffron and olive oil.

Rissole, this term when pertaining to meats means to sear or brown with a protective crust. In regard to cakes, fritters, etc., it means to coat them with a golden brown crust.

Roulade, this is the more general name for *Pauppiette.*

Royales, see No. 213.

Salamander, this is a large sheet of iron on which are heaped red hot coals, so that if one holds this against a dish it browns or glazes it, almost at once. A clean coal shovel may be used for the same purpose. See Drawing.

Salpicon, a compound of various products, cut into dice and generally combined with a sauce or a forcemeat.

Sauté, see No. 251.

Savarin Mould, see Drawing.

Soufflé, a name given to a class of light, hot or cold preparations of fish, meat, poultry, etc. Also to sweets to which the whites of eggs are added if the preparation is served hot, and to which whipped cream is added if it is served cold.

Spring-Form, see Drawing.

Star Mould, see Drawing.

Swashing or Swirling, when referred to, it actually means scraping from the utensil used the adhered particles and diluting it with the wine or liquid indicated in the recipe.

Stud or Lard, studding is done by injecting protruding pieces of fat into the incisions made in the meat with a sharp knife. Larding uses the same strip of fat or bacon, which are inserted into a larding needle. With this, one pinches the meat at regular intervals allowing the larding fat to show at the point of its entry. See Drawing.

Subrics are really spinach puffs.

Supreme, this is the name given to the fillet or the breast of fowl. The term has

Tart Mould, see Drawing.

Tartlet Mould, see Drawing.

Tazza Mould, Fancy cup mould.

Terrine, this is a patty and its container. But a terrine à pâté is an earthenware dish in which a patty or food is cooked. See Drawing.

Timbale, may mean a *Timbale* Mould and it may mean a food cooked in the Mould or crust, and formed in such a manner. See Drawing.

Verjuice, this is the juice of unripe fruit, such as grapes, etc. Sometimes used as a substitute for vinegar in acidulating water.

Vesiga is the dried spine-marrow of the sturgeon and very difficult to procure.

Zest, the outermost, colored glossy film of the rind of an orange or lemon.

CHAPTER I

BASIC PRINCIPLES OF COOKERY

BEFORE undertaking the description of the different kinds of dishes whose recipes I intend giving in this work, it will be necessary to reveal the groundwork whereon these recipes are built. And, although this has already been done again and again, and is wearisome in the extreme, a text-book on cooking that did not include it would be not only incomplete, but in many cases incomprehensible.

Notwithstanding the fact that it is the usual procedure, in culinary matters, to insist upon the importance of the part played by stock, I feel compelled to refer to it at the outset of this work, and to lay even further stress upon what has already been written on the subject.

Indeed, stock is everything in cooking, at least in French cooking. Without it, nothing can be done. If one's stock is good, what remains of the work is easy; if, on the other hand, it is bad or merely mediocre, it is quite hopeless to expect anything approaching a satisfactory result.

The cook mindful of success, therefore, will naturally direct his attention to the faultless preparation of his stock, and, in order to achieve this result, he will find it necessary not merely to make use of the freshest and finest products, but also to exercise the most scrupulous care in their preparation, for, in cooking, care is half the battle. Unfortunately, no theories, no formulæ, and no recipes, however well written, can take the place of practical experience in the acquisition of a full knowledge concerning this part of the work—the most important, the most essential, and certainly the most difficult part.

1

In the matter of stock it is, above all, necessary to have a sufficient quantity of the finest materials at one's disposal. Every cook knows this, and any master or mistress of a house who stints in this respect forfeits the right to make any remark whatsoever to the *chef* concerning his work, for, let the talent or merits of the latter be what they may, they are crippled by insufficient or inferior material. It is just as absurd to exact excellent cooking from a *chef* whom one provides with defective or scanty goods, as to hope to obtain wine from a bottled decoction of logwood.

The Principal Kinds of Fonds de Cuisine (Foundation Sauces and Stocks)

The principal kinds of fonds de cuisine are:—

1. Ordinary and clarified consommés.
2. The brown stock or *"estouffade,"* game stocks, the bases of thickened gravies and of brown sauces.
3. White stock, basis of white sauces.
4. Fish stock.
5. The various essences of poultry, game, fish, &c., the complements of small sauces.
6. The various *glazes:* meat, game and poultry.
7. The basic sauces: Espagnole, Velouté, Béchamel, Tomato, and Hollandaise.
8. The savory jellies or aspics of old-fashioned cooking.

To these kinds of stock, which, in short, represent the buttresses of the culinary edifice, must now be added the following preparations, which are, in a measure, the auxiliaries of the above:—

1. The *roux,* the thickening element in sauces.
2. The *"Mirepoix"* and *"Matignon"* aromatic and flavoring elements.
3. The *"Court-Bouillon"* and the *"Blancs."*
4. The various stuffings.
5. The *marinades.*
6. The various garnishes for soups, for *relevés,* for entrées, &c. ("Duxelle," "Duchesse," "Dauphine," *Pâte à choux,* frying batters, various *Salpicons, Profiteroles, Royales,* Œufs filés, *Diablotins,* Pastes, Dough or Batters, etc.).

1—ORDINARY OR WHITE CONSOMME   *Fonds Blancs Ordinaires*

Quantities for making Four Quarts

3 lbs. of shin of beef.
3 lbs. of lean beef.
1½ lbs. of fowls' skeletons.
1 lb. of carrots.
½ lb. of turnips.

¾ lb. of leeks and 1 stalk of celery.
¼ lb. of parsnips.
1 medium-sized onion with a clove stuck in it.

Preparation.—Put the meat into a stock-pot of suitable dimensions, after having previously tied it together; add the fowl skeletons, five quarts of water, and one-half oz. of table salt. Place the stock-pot on a moderate fire in such a manner that it may not boil too quickly, and remember to stir the meat from time to time. Under the influence of the heat, the water gradually reaches the interior of the meat, where, after having dissolved the liquid portions, it eventually combines with them. These liquid portions contain a large proportion of albumen, and as the temperature of the water rises this substance has a tendency to coagulate. It also increases in volume, and, by virtue of its lightness, escapes from the water and accumulates on the surface in the form of scum. Carefully remove this scum as it forms, and occasionally add a little cold water before the boil is reached in order that, the latter being retarded, a complete expulsion of the scum may be effected. The clearness of the consommé largely depends upon the manner in which this skimming has been carried out. Then the vegetable garnishing is added. The scum from this is removed as in the previous case, and the edge of the stock-pot should be carefully wiped to the level of the fluid, so as to free it from the deposit which has formed there. The stock-pot is then moved to a corner of the fire where it may continue cooking slowly for four or five hours. At the end of this time it should be taken immediately from the fire, and, after half a pint of cold water has been added to its contents, it should be left to rest a few minutes to permit the grease to accumulate on the surface of the liquid, whence it must be carefully removed before the consommé is strained. This last operation is effected by means of a very fine strainer, placed on the top of a white tureen (clean and wide), which should be chilled to hasten the cooling of the consommé. The tureen should not on any account be covered, and this more particularly in summer, when rapid cooling is a precautionary measure against fermentation.

Remarks upon the Different Causes which Combine to Influence the Quality of a Consommé

It will be seen that I have not made any mention in the above recipe of the meat and the vegetables which have helped to make the consommé, my reason being that it is preferable to remove them from the stock-pot only after the broth has been strained, so as not to run the risk of disturbing the latter.

The quality of the meat goes a long way towards establishing the quality of the consommé. In order that the latter be perfect, it is essential that the meat used should be that of comparatively old animals whose flesh is well set and rich in flavor.

Now to extract that gelatinous element from bone which produces the mellowness characteristic of all good consommés, it is necessary that the gelatigenous bodies should be cooked for twelve hours at least, and even after that time has elapsed they are still not entirely spent.

I therefore believe that, in the case of either consommé or stock, the recipe of which I shall give later, it would be advisable for the bones to stew at least twelve hours, and this only after they have been well broken up, while the quantity of water used should be sufficient to allow exactly for the immersion of the meat that must follow. The contents of this first stock-pot should include half of the vegetables mentioned, and the consommé thus obtained, after having been strained and cooled, will take the place of the water in the recipe, in accordance with the directions I have given above.

The Uses of White Consommé

White consommé is used in the preparation of clarified consommés, in which case it undergoes a process of clearing, the directions for which will be given later. It also serves as the liquor for thick soups, poached fowls, etc. It must be transparent, as colorless as possible, and very slightly salted, for, whatever the use may be for which it is intended, it has to undergo a process of concentration.

2—THE PREPARATION OF CLARIFIED CONSOMME FOR CLEAR SOUPS   *La Préparation des Fonds Clarifiés*

Quantities for making four quarts.—Five quarts of ordinary consommé, one and one-half lbs. of very lean beef, the white of an egg, one fowl's skeleton (roasted if possible). First, mince the beef and put through a grinder with the fowl's skeleton and the white of egg, adding a little cold white consommé. Put the whole into a tall, narrow, and thick-bottomed saucepan or pot; then gradually add the cold, white broth, from which all grease has been removed, that the whole may be well mixed. Then the pot may be put on the fire, and its contents thoroughly stirred, to prevent their burning at the bottom. When boiling-point almost is reached, move the saucepan to a corner of the fire, so that the soup may only simmer, for anything approaching the boil would disturb the contents. A good hour should be enough to complete the consommé, and any longer time on the fire would be rather injurious than helpful, as it would probably impair the flavor of the preparation. Now carefully remove what little grease may have collected on the surface of the consommé, and strain the latter through muslin into another clean saucepan. It is now ready for the addition of the garnishes that are to form part of it, which I shall enumerate in due course.

Remarks upon Clarifications

For clarified consommés, even more than for the ordinary kind, it is eminently advisable that the meat should be that of old animals. Indeed, it is safe to say that one lb. of meat coming from an animal of eight years will yield much better consommé than two lbs. would, coming from a fattened animal of about three or four years. The consommé will be stronger, mellower, and certainly more tasty, as the flesh of young animals has absolutely no richness of flavor.

It will be seen that I do not refer to any vegetable for the clarification. If the white consommé has been well carried out, it should be able to dispense with all supplementary flavoring, and, the customary error of cooks being rather to overdo the quantity of vegetables—even to the extent of disguising the natural aroma of the consommé—I preferred to entirely abandon the idea of vegetable garnishes in clarifications, and thus avoid a common stumbling-block.

3—CHICKEN CONSOMME   *Fonds de Volaille*

White chicken consommé is prepared in exactly the same way as ordinary white consommé. There need only be added to the meat, the quantity of which may be lessened, an old hen or a cock, slightly browned on the spit or in the oven.

For the clarification, the quantity of roast fowl skeletons used may be increased, provided the latter be not too fat. The process, however, is the same as in the clarification of ordinary consommés.

The color of chicken consommé should be lighter than that of the ordinary kind—namely, a light, amber yellow, transparent and warm.

4—FISH CONSOMME   *Fonds de Poisson*

These consommés are rarely used, for *Lenten* soups with a fish basis are generally thick soups, for the preparation of which the fish *fumet* (Recipe 11) should avail. Whenever there is no definite reason for the use of an absolutely *Lenten* consommé, it would be advisable to resort to one of the ordinary kind, and to finish off the same by means of a good fish essence extracted from the bones of a sole of whiting. An excellent consommé is thus obtained, more palatable and less flat than the plain fish consommé.

If, however, one were obliged to make a plain fish consommé, the following procedure should be adopted:—

Clarification of Fish Consommé

Quantities for making Four Quarts.—Four and one-half quarts of ordinary fish *fumet* having a decided taste; one-half lb. of good caviar, or pressed caviar.

Mode of Procedure.—Pound the caviar and mix the pulp with the cold fish *fumet*. Put the whole into a saucepan, place it on the fire, and stir with a spatula until the contents reach the boil. Then move the saucepan to a corner of the fire. and let the consommé simmer gently for twenty minutes, after which strain it through muslin with great caution, and keep it well covered and in the warmth, to prevent the formation of a gelatinous film on the surface.

Fish consommés are greatly improved by the addition of such aromatics as saffron or curry, both of which considerably add to their quality.

5—GAME CONSOMME   *Fonds de Gibier*

The necks, breasts, and shoulders of venison and of hare, old wild rabbits, old pheasants, and old partridges may be used in the production of game consommés. An ordinary consommé may likewise be made, in which half the beef can be replaced by veal, and to which may be added, while clarifying, a succulent game *essence*. This last method is even preferable when dealing with game birds, but in either case it is essential that the meat used should be half-roasted beforehand, in order to strengthen the *fumet*.

The recipe that I give below must therefore only be looked upon as a model, necessarily alterable according to the resources at one's disposal, the circumstances, and the end in view.

Quantities for making Four Quarts of Plain Game Consommé.

3 lbs. of neck, shoulder, or breast of venison.	1 medium-sized leek and 2 stalks of celery.
1½ lbs. of hare-trimmings.	1 herb bunch with extra thyme and bay leaves.
1 old pheasant or 2 partridges.	
4 oz. of sliced carrots, browned in butter.	1 onion, oven-browned, with 2 cloves stuck into it.
½ lb. of mushrooms browned in butter.	

Liquor.—Five and one-half quarts of water.

Seasoning.—One oz. of salt and a few peppercorns, these to be added ten minutes previous to straining the consommé.

Time allowed for cooking.—Three hours.

Mode of Procedure.—Proceed in exactly the same way as for ordinary consommés (1), taking care only to half-roast the meat, as I pointed out above, before putting it in the saucepan.

THE CLARIFICATION OF GAME CONSOMMÉS

The ingredients of the clarification of game consommés vary according to the kind desired. If it is to have a partridge flavor, one partridge should be allowed for each quart of the consommé, whereas if its flavor is to be that of the pheasant, half an old pheasant will be required per each quart of the liquid. Last, in the case of plain game consommés, one lb. of lean venison, hare, or wild rabbit should be allowed for each quart required.

Mode of Procedure.—Whatever be the kind of game used, the latter must be thoroughly boned and the meat well ground, together with the white of an egg per four quarts of consommé. About two oz. per quart of dried mushrooms should now be added if they can be procured, while the bones and the meat of the game should be browned in the oven and completely drained of all grease. The whole can now be mixed with the cold game consommé (5). The clarification is then put over a fire (stirring constantly), and as soon as the boil is reached the saucepan must be moved to a corner of the fire, where its contents may gently boil for three-quarters of an hour longer. The fat should then be removed, and the consommé strained through muslin, after which cover until wanted

6—SPECIAL CONSOMME FOR SUPPERS   *Potages pour les Soupers*

The consommés whose recipes I have just given are intended more particularly for dinners. They are always finished off by some kind of garnish, which, besides lending them an additional touch of flavor, gives them their special and definite character when they are served.

But the case is otherwise with the consommés served for suppers. These, being only served in cups, either hot or cold, do not allow for any garnishing, since they are to be drunk at table. They must therefore be perfect in themselves, delicate, and quite clear.

These special consommés are made in a similar manner to the others, though it is needful to slightly increase the quantity of meat used for the clarification, and to add to that clarification the particular flavor mentioned on the menu—to wit, a few stalks of celery, if the consommé is that type; a small quantity of curry, if the consommé is made "à l'Indienne"; or a few old roast partridges if it is to be termed "Consommé au *fumet* de perdreau"; and so on.

The means by which one may vary the aroma of consommés are legion, but it is highly important, whatever aroma used, that it be not too pronounced. It should only lend a distinctive and, at the same time, subtle finish to the consommé, which, besides sharpening the latter, should increase its succulence.

When the consommé is served cold it ought to have the qualities of an extremely light and easily-melting jelly, barely firm; but when it is too liquid, it rarely gives that sensation of perfection and succulence to the palate of the consumer which the latter expects. When too firm and too gelatinous it is positively disagreeable; therefore, if it is to be relished, it should be of just the right consistency.

7—BROWN STOCK OR ESTOUFFADE   *Fonds Brun ou Estouffade*

Quantities for making Four Quarts

4 lbs. of shin of beef (flesh and bone).

4 lbs. of shin of veal (flesh and bone).

½ lb. of lean, raw ham.

½ lb. of fresh pork rind, *blanched.*

¾ lb. of minced carrots, browned in butter.

¾ lb. of minced onions, browned in butter.

1 herb bunch, containing a little parsley, a stalk of celery, a small sprig of thyme, and a bay leaf.

Preparation.—Bone and tie the meat, and keep it handy. Break the bones as finely as possible, and, after having sprinkled them with a little stock-fat, brown them in an oven; also stir them repeatedly. When they are slightly browned, put them in a conveniently large saucepan with the carrots, the onions, and the herb bunch. Add five quarts of cold water, and put the saucepan on to boil. As soon as the boil is reached skim carefully; wipe the edge of the saucepan; put the lid half on, and allow the stock to cook gently for twelve hours; then roughly remove the fat; strain the liquid through a sieve, and let it cool.

This being done, put the meat in a saucepan just large enough to hold it. Brown it a little in some stock-fat and drain off fat entirely. Add half a pint of the prepared stock, cover the saucepan, and let the meat simmer on the side of the fire until the stock is almost entirely reduced. Meanwhile the meat should have been repeatedly turned, that it may be equally affected throughout. Now pour the remainder of the stock, prepared from bones, into the saucepan, bring the whole to a boil, and continue very slowly and regularly with the lid off. As soon as the meat is well cooked the fat should be removed from the stock, and it should be strained or rubbed through a sieve, after which it should be put aside to be used when required.

Remarks Relative to the Making of Brown Stock.—Instead of tying the meat after having boned it, if time presses, it may be cut into large cubes before browning. In this case one hour and a half would suffice to cook it and to extract all its juice.

Whether brown or white, stock should never be salted, because it is never served in its original state. It is either reduced in order to make *glazes* or sauces—in which case the concentration answers the purpose of seasoning—or else it is used to cook meat which must be salted before being cooked and which, therefore, imparts the necessary salt to its surrounding liquor.

Brown stock ought to be the color of fine burnt amber, and it must be transparent. It is used in making meat *glazes* (14) after reduction, also to moisten meat for *braising* and to prepare brown sauces.

8—BROWN GAME STOCK   *Fonds de Gibier Brun*

There is no difference between the game consommés and game stock, or, otherwise stated, ordinary game consommé and brown game stock are one and the same thing. The distinction lies in the ultimate use of this preparation; it is clarified, as we have shown (5), if it be intended for a clear soup, and it is used in its original state if it is to be used for a thick game soup, for a sauce, or for reducing.

9—BROWN VEAL STOCK   *Fonds de Veau Brun*

Brown veal stock requires the same quantities of shin and trimmings of veal as white veal stock (10). The time allowed for cooking is, however, a little shorter, and this operation may be completed within eight hours. This stock is mostly used as the liquor for poultry and *poëled* game, while it may also serve in the preparation of thickened veal stock. Being quite neutral in taste, it lends itself to all purposes, and readily takes up the aroma of the meat with which it may happen to be combined. It is admirably suited to the *poaching* of quails, and nothing can supplant it in this particular.

10—WHITE VEAL STOCK AND POULTRY STOCK
Fonds de Veau Blanc et de Volaille

Quantities for making Four Quarts

8 lbs. of shin of veal, or lean and fresh veal trimmings.

1 or 2 fowls' skeletons, uncooked if they are handy.

12 oz. of carrots.

6 oz. of onions stuck with a clove.

5½ quarts of cold water.

4 oz. of leeks tied with a stalk of celery.

1 herb bunch, including 1 oz. of parsley, 1 bay leaf, and a small sprig of thyme.

Preparation.—Bone the shins, string the meat, break up the bones as small as possible, and put them in a saucepan with the water. Place on an open fire, allow to boil, skim carefully, and then move to a side of the fire to cook very gently for five hours. At the end of this time put the stock into another saucepan, add the meat and the vegetables, add water, if necessary, to keep the quantity of liquid at five quarts, let it boil, and allow it to cook slowly for another three hours, after which remove all grease from the stock, pass it through a fine strainer or a colander, and put it aside until wanted.

Remarks upon White Stock.—One should contrive to make this stock as gelatinous as possible. It is therefore an indispensable measure that the bones be well broken up and cooked for at least eight hours. Veal never yields such clear stock as beef; nevertheless, the consommé obtained from veal should not be cloudy. It must, on the contrary, be kept as clear and as white as possible.

Poultry Stock is made by adding two old fowls to the above veal stock, and these should be put into the liquor with the meat.

Fish Stock

11—WHITE FISH STOCK   *Fumet Blanc de Poisson*

Quantities for making Four Quarts

4 lbs. of trimmings and bones of sole or whiting.
½ lb. of sliced *blanched* onions.

2 oz. of parsley root or stalks.
½ bottle of white wine.

Preparation.—Butter the bottom of a thick, deep saucepan, put in the *blanched* onions and the parsley-stalks, and upon these lay the fish remains. Add the juice of a lemon, cover the saucepan, put it on the fire, and allow the fish to exude its essence, shaking the pan at intervals. Moisten, in the first place, with the white wine; then, with the lid off, reduce the liquid to about half. Now add four quarts of cold water, bring to a boil, skim, and then leave to cook for twenty minutes, only, on a moderate fire. The time allowed is ample for the purpose of extracting the aromatic and gelatinous properties contained in the bones, and a lengthened stewing would only impair the savor of the stock.

Remarks upon White Fish Stock.—The recipe which I give above diverges considerably from that commonly used, for, as a rule, fish stock is diluted far too much, and is cooked for much too long a time. I have observed that fish stock may be greatly improved by rapid cooking, and it was this consideration that led me to dilute it scantily, so as to avoid prolonged reduction.

It is likewise necessary to remember that in order to make perfect fish stock, only the sole or whiting should be used. In a case of emergency, however, if the supply of the latter were to run short, a quarter of their weight of turbot bones might be added to them. But all other kinds of fish should be avoided in the preparation.

12—FISH STOCK WITH RED WINE   *Fumet de Poisson au Vin Rouge*

This stock is comparatively rarely used, because, in practice, it is naturally obtained in the cooking of the fish itself, as, for instance, in the case of the *"Matelotes"* (1037). Be this as it may, with the recent invasion of a custom which seems to demand, ever more and more, the serving of fish without bones, the following recipe will be worthy of interest, as it is likely that its need will henceforth be felt with increasing urgency.

Fish *fumet* with red wine may be prepared from all fresh-water fish, as well as from the remains of sole, whiting, chicken-turbot, and turbot. It is generally better, however, to have recourse to the bones and remains of that fish which happens to be constituting the dish —that is to say, the bones and trimmings of sole in a stock for fillet of sole, the bones and trimmings of a chicken-turbot in a *fumet* for a chicken-turbot, and so on. The preparatory recipe remains the same, whatever kind of fish used may be.

Quantities for making Four Quarts of Fumet with Red Wine.— Four lbs. of bones, heads, and trimmings of the fish to be served; three-quarters lb. of minced white onions; three oz. of parsley stalks, two bay leaves, four small sprigs of thyme, and four cloves of garlic; two bottles of red wine and four pints of water.

Mode of Procedure.—Put all the above-mentioned ingredients in a heavy and deep saucepan, boil, skim carefully, and allow to cook twenty to thirty minutes on a moderate fire; then strain the stock through a colander into a tureen, to be used when required.

Remarks upon Fish Stock with Red Wine.—This stock stands reduction far better than white fish stock. Nevertheless, I urge the advisability of trying to obtain the required quantity without too much cooking. In its preparation, one may use some mushroom peelings, as in the case of white stock, if these are handy, and they will be found to lend an agreeable flavor to the fish *fumet*.

13—VARIOUS ESSENCES   *Essences Diverses*

As their name implies, *essences* are stock which hold a large proportion of a substance's aroma in a concentrated form. They are, in fact, ordinary stock, only less diluted, with the idea of intensifying the flavor of the treated ingredients; hence their utility is *nil* if the stock which they are intended to complete has been properly treated. It is infinitely simpler to make savory and succulent stock in the first place than to produce a mediocre stock, and finally complete it by a specially prepared *essence*. The result in the first instance is better, and there is economy of time and material.

The most one can do is to recommend, in certain circumstances, the use of essences extracted from particularly well-flavored products, as, for instance, mushrooms, truffles, morels, and celery. But it would be well to remember that, nine times out of ten, it is preferable to add the product itself to the stock during the preparation of the same rather than to prepare *essences*.

For this reason I do not think it necessary to enlarge upon the subject of *essences*, the need of which should not be felt in good cooking.

14—VARIOUS GLAZES

The various *glazes* of meat, fowl, game, and fish are merely stock reduced to the point of glutinous consistency. Their uses are legion. Occasionally they serve in decorating dishes with a brilliant and smooth coating which makes them appetizing; at other times they may help to strengthen the consistency of a sauce or other culinary preparation, while again they may be used as sauces proper after they have been correctly creamed or buttered.

Glazes are distinguished from *essences* by the fact that the latter are only prepared with the object of extracting all the flavor of the product under treatment, whereas the former are, on the contrary, constituted by the whole base of the substance itself. They therefore have not only its savor, but also its succulence and mellowness, whereby they are superior to the *essences*, and cooking can but be improved by substituting them for the latter. Nevertheless, many *chefs* of the old school do not permit the use of *glazes* in culinary preparations, or, rather, they are of opinion that each cooking operation should produce them on its own account, and thus be sufficient unto itself. Certainly, the theory is correct when neither time nor cost is limited. But nowadays the establishments are scarce where these theories may be applied, and, indeed, if one does not make an abuse of *glazes,* and if they be prepared with care, their use gives excellent results, while they lend themselves admirably to the very complex demands of modern customs.

15—MEAT GLAZE   *Glace de Viande*

Meat *glaze* is made by reducing brown stock (7) in a large saucepan upon an open fire. As often as the stock is appreciably reduced, during boiling, it may be transferred to smaller pots, taking care to strain it through muslin at each change. The *glaze* may be considered sufficiently reduced when it evenly coats a withdrawn spoon. The fire used for reducing should gradually diminish as the concentration progresses, and the last phase must be done slowly and on a moderate fire.

When it is necessary to obtain a lighter and clearer *glaze,* the brown veal stock (9) should be reduced instead of the *"Estouffade."*

16—POULTRY GLAZE   *Glace de Volaille*

Reduce the poultry base indicated in (10), and proceed in exactly the same way as for meat *glaze* (15).

17—GAME GLAZE   *Glace de Gibier*

Use the game base (8), and proceed as for meat *glaze* (15).

18—FISH GLAZE   *Glace de Poisson*

This *glaze* is used less often than the preceding ones. As it is only used to intensify the savor of sauces, it is sufficient for this purpose to prepare a white fish stock (11), which may be diluted with the stock already prepared, and which may be reduced according to the requirements. The name of fish *fumet* or fish *essence* is given to this preparation; its flavor is more delicate than that of fish *glaze,* which it replaces with advantage.

CHAPTER II

WARM sauces are of two kinds: the leading sauces, also called "mother sauces," and the small sauces, which are usually derived from the first-named, and are generally only modified forms. Cooking stock only includes the leading sauces, but I shall refer to the small hot sauces and the cold sauces at the end of the auxiliary stock.

Experience, which plays such an important part in culinary work, is nowhere so necessary as in the preparation of sauces, for not only must the latter flatter the palate, but they must also vary in savor, consistency and viscosity, in accordance with the dishes they accompany. By this means, in a well-ordered dinner, each dish differs from the preceding ones and from those that follow.

Furthermore, sauces must, through the perfection of their preparation, obey the general laws of a rational hygiene, wherefore they should be served and combined in such a way as to allow for easy digestion by the frequently disordered stomachs of their consumers.

Carême was quite justified in priding himself upon the fact that during his stay at the English Court his master—the Prince Regent —had assured him that he (Carême) was the only one among those who had served his Highness whose cooking had been at all easy to digest. Carême had grasped the essential truth that the richer the cooking is, the more speedily do the stomach and palate tire of it. And, indeed, it is a great mistake to suppose that, in order to do good cooking, it is necessary to be extravagant in one's use of all things. In reality, practice dictates fixed and regular quantities, and from these one cannot diverge without upsetting the hygienic and taste balance on which the value of a sauce depends. The requisite quantities of each ingredient must, of course, be used, but neither more nor less, as there are objections to either extreme.

Any sauce whatsoever should be smooth, light (without being liquid), glossy to the eye, and decided in taste. When these conditions are fulfilled it is always easy to digest even for tired stomachs.

An essential point in the making of sauces is the seasoning, and it would be impossible for me to lay sufficient stress on the importance of not indulging in any excess in this respect. It too often happens that the insipidity of a badly-made sauce is corrected by excessive seasoning; this is an absolutely deplorable practice.

Seasoning should be so calculated as to be merely a complementary factor, which, though it must throw the savor of dishes into relief, may not form a recognizable part of them. If it be excessive, it modifies and even destroys the taste peculiar to every dish—to the great detriment of the latter and of the consumer's health.

It is therefore desirable that each sauce should possess its own special flavor, well defined, the result of the combined flavors of all its ingredients.

THE ROUX

The *roux* being the thickening element of leading sauces, it is necessary to reveal its preparation and ingredients before giving one's attention to the latter.

Three kinds of *roux* are used—namely, brown *roux,* for brown sauces; pale *roux,* for veloutés, or cream sauces; and white *roux,* for white sauces and Béchamel.

19—BROWN ROUX   *Roux Brun*

Quantities for making about One lb.—Eight oz. of clarified butter (175), nine oz. of best-quality flour.

Preparation.—Mix the flour and butter in a very thick saucepan, and put it on the side of the fire or in a moderate oven. Stir the mixture repeatedly so that the heat may be evenly distributed throughout.

The time allowed for the cooking of brown *roux* cannot be precisely determined, as it depends upon the degree of heat employed. The more intense the latter, the more speedy will be the cooking, while the stirring will of necessity be more rapid. Brown *roux* is known to be cooked when it has acquired a fine, light brown color and when it exudes an odor resembling that of the hazel-nut, characteristic of baked flour.

It is very important that brown *roux* should not be cooked too rapidly. As a matter of fact, among the various constituent elements of flour, the starch alone acts as the binding principle. This starch is contained in little cells, which tightly constrain it, but which are sufficiently porous to permit the percolation of liquid and fatty substances. Under the influence of moderate heat and the infiltered butter, the cells burst through the swelling of the starch, and the latter thereupon completely combines with the butter to form a mass capable of absorbing six times its own weight of liquid when cooked.

When the cooking takes place with a very high heat in the beginning the starch gets burned within its shrivelled cells, and swelling is then possible only in those parts which have been least burned.

The binding principle is thus destroyed, and double or treble the quantity of *roux* becomes necessary in order to obtain the required consistency. But this excess of *roux* in the sauce chokes it up without binding it, and prevents it from clearing. At the same time, the cellulose and the burnt starch lend a bitterness to the sauce of which no subsequent treatment can rid it.

From the above it follows that, starch being the only one from among the different constituents of flour which really affects the thickening of sauces, there would be considerable advantage in preparing *roux* either from a pure form of it, or from substances with kindred properties, such as *fecula,* arrowroot, cornstarch, etc. It is only habit that causes flour to be still used as the binding element of *roux,* and, indeed, the hour is not so far distant when the advantages of the changes I propose will be better understood—changes which have been already recommended by Favre in his dictionary.

With a *roux* well made from the purest starch—in which case the volume of starch and butter would equal about half that of the flour and butter of the old method—and with strong and succulent brown stock, a Spanish sauce or Espagnole may be made in one hour. And this sauce will be clearer, more brilliant, and better than that of the old processes, which needed three days at least to throw off the scum.

20—PALE ROUX *Roux Blond*

The quantities are the same as for brown *roux,* but cooking must cease as soon as the color of the *roux* begins to change, and before the appearance of any coloring whatsoever.

The observations I made relative to brown *roux,* concerning the thickening element, apply also to pale *roux.*

21—WHITE ROUX   *Roux Blanc*

Same quantities as for brown (19) and pale *roux* (20), but the time of cooking is limited to a few minutes, as it is only needful, in this case, to do away with the disagreeable taste of flour which is typical of those sauces whose *roux* has not been sufficiently cooked.

22—BROWN SAUCE OR ESPAGNOLE SAUCE

Sauce Brun ou Sauce Espagnole

Quantities Required for Four Quarts.—One lb. of brown (19) *roux* dissolved in a deep, thick saucepan with six quarts of brown stock (7) or estouffade. Put the saucepan on an open fire, and stir the sauce with a spatula or a whisk, and do not stop until it begins to boil. Then remove the whisk, and put the saucepan on a corner of the fire, letting it lean slightly to one side with the help of a wedge, so that boiling may only take place at one point, and that the scum thrown out by the sauce may accumulate high up in the saucepan, whence they can be easily removed as they collect.

It is advisable during the skimming to change saucepans twice or even three times, straining every time, and adding a quart of brown stock (7) to replace what has evaporated. At length, when the sauce begins to get lighter, and about two hours before finally straining it, two lbs. of fresh tomatoes, roughly cut up, should be added, or an equivalent quantity of tomato purée, and about one lb. of *Mirepoix* (228). The sauce is then reduced so as to measure four quarts when strained, after which it is poured into a wide tureen, and must be kept in motion until quite cool lest a skin should form on its surface.

The time required for the skimming of an Espagnole varies according to the quality of the stock and *roux.* We saw above that one hour sufficed for a concentrated stock and starch *roux,* in which case the *Mirepoix* and the tomato are added from the first. But much more time is required if one is dealing with a *roux* whose base is flour. In the latter case six hours should be allowed, provided one have excellent stock and well-made *roux.* More often than not this work is done in two stages, thus: after having skimmed the Espagnole for six or eight hours the first day, it is put on the fire the next day with half its volume of stock, and it is left to settle a few hours more before it is finally strained.

Summing up my opinion on this subject, I can only give cooks the following advice, based upon long experience:—

1. Only use strong, clear stock with a decided taste.

2. Be scrupulously careful of the *roux,* however it may be made. By following these two rules, a clear, brilliant, and consistent Espagnole will always be obtained in a fairly short time.

23—HALF GLAZE   *Demi-Glace*

This is the Espagnole sauce, having reached the limit of perfection by final skimming. It is obtained by reducing one quart of Espagnole and one quart of first-class brown stock (7) until its volume is reduced to nine-tenths of a quart. It is then strained into a double-boiler of convenient dimensions, and it is finished, away from the fire, with one-tenth of a quart of excellent sherry. Cover the double-boiler, or slightly butter the top to avoid the formation of a skin. This sauce is the base of all the smaller brown sauces.

24—LENTEN ESPAGNOLE   *Espagnole Maigre*

Practical men are not agreed as to the need of *Lenten* Espagnole. The ordinary Espagnole being really a neutral sauce in flavor, it is quite simple to give it the necessary flavor by the addition of the required quantity of fish *fumet.* It is only, therefore, when one wishes to conform with the demands of a genuine Lent sauce that a fish Espagnole is needed. And, certainly in this case, nothing can take its place.

The preparation of this Espagnole does not differ from that of the ordinary kind, except that the bacon is replaced by mushroom peelings in the *Mirepoix,* and that the sauce must be skimmed for only one hour.

This sauce takes the place of the ordinary Espagnole, for *Lenten* preparations, in every case where the latter is generally used, in *Gratins,* in the Genevoise sauce, etc.

25—ORDINARY VELOUTE SAUCE   *Velouté (Sauce Blanche)*

Quantities Required for Four Quarts.—One lb. of pale *roux* (20), five quarts of white veal stock (10).

Dissolve the *roux* in the cold white veal stock and put the saucepan containing this mixture on an open fire, stirring the sauce with a spatula or whisk, so as to avoid its burning at the bottom. Add one oz. of table-salt, a pinch of nutmeg and white powdered pepper, together with one-quarter lb. of nice white mushroom peelings, if these are handy. Now boil and move to a corner of the fire to scum slowly for one and a half hours, at the same time observing the precautions advised for ordinary Espagnole (22). Strain through muslin into a smaller saucepan, add one pint of white stock, and allow to settle for another half hour. Strain it again through a fine sieve into a wide tureen, and keep stirring it with a spatula until it is quite cold.

I am not partial to garnishing Velouté Sauce with carrots, an onion with a clove stuck into it, and an herb bunch, as many do. The stock should be sufficiently fragrant itself, without requiring the addition of anything beyond the usual condiments. The only exception I should make would be for mushroom peelings, even though it is preferable, when possible, to replace these by mushroom liquor. But this is always scarce in kitchens where it is used for other purposes; wherefore it is often imperative to have recourse to mushrooms instead. The latter may not, however, be added to the stock itself, as they would blacken it; hence I advise their addition to the Velouté during its preparation.

26—CHICKEN VELOUTE   *Velouté de Volaille*

This is identical with ordinary Velouté, except that instead of having white veal stock (10) for its liquor, it is diluted with white poultry stock (10). The mode of procedure and the time allowed for cooking are the same.

26a—FISH VELOUTE   *Velouté de Poisson*

Velouté is the base of various fish sauces.

Prepare it in precisely the same way as poultry velouté, but instead of using poultry stock, use very clear fish *fumet,* and let it scum for twenty minutes only. (See fish *fumet* No. 11.)

27—THICKENED VELOUTE   *Sauce Allemande*

Allemande Sauce or thickened Velouté is not, strictly speaking, a basic sauce. However, it is so often resorted to in the preparation of other sauces that I think it necessary to give it after the Veloutés, from which it is derived.

Quantities Required for One Quart

The yolks of 5 eggs.
1 pint of cold white stock (1).
1 quart of Velouté (25), well
    cleared.

½ the juice of a lemon.
¼ pint of mushroom liquor.

Mode of Procedure.—Put the various ingredients in a thick-bottomed saucepan and mix them carefully. Then put the pan on an open fire, and stir the sauce with a metal spatula, lest it burn at the bottom. When the sauce has been reduced to about one quart, add one-third pint of fresh cream to it, and reduce further for a few minutes. It should then be passed through a fine strainer into a tureen and kept agitated until quite cold.

Prepared thus, the Allemande Sauce is ready for the preparation of the smaller sauces. Butter must only be added at the very last moment, for if it were buttered any earlier it would most surely separate. The same holds true with this sauce when it is to be served in its original state; it should then receive a small addition of cream, and be buttered so that it may attain its required delicacy; but this addition of butter and cream ought only to be made at the last moment, and away from the fire. When a sauce thickened with egg yolks has any fat substance added to it, it cannot be exposed to a higher temperature than 140 degrees Fahrenheit without risking curdling.

28—BECHAMEL SAUCE   *Sauce Béchamel*

Quantities Required for Four Quarts

1 lb. of white *roux* (21).	⅔ oz. of salt, 1 pinch of *mignon-*
4½ quarts of boiling milk.	*ette* pepper, and grated nut-
½ lb. of lean veal.	meg, and 1 small sprig of
	thyme.
	1 minced onion.

Preparation.—Pour the boiling milk on the *roux,* which should be almost cold, and whisk it well to avoid lumping. Let it boil, then cook on the side of the fire. Meanwhile the lean veal should have been cut into small cubes, and fried with butter in a saucepan, together with the minced onion. When the veal has cooked without becoming browned, it is added to the Béchamel, together with salt and the other seasonings. Let the sauce boil slowly for about one hour in all, and then strain it through a fine sieve into a tureen; butter the top, lest a crust should form.

When Béchamel is intended for *Lenten* preparations, the veal must be omitted.

There is another way of making the sauce. After having boiled the milk, the seasoning and herbs should be added; the saucepan is then covered and placed on a corner of the stove, so as to ensure a thorough infusion. The boiling milk must now be poured on to the *roux* which has been separately prepared, and the sauce should then cook for one quarter of an hour only.

29—TOMATO SAUCE   *Sauce Tomatée*

Quantities Required for Four Quarts

5 oz. of salt pork, rather fat.
6 oz. of carrots cut into cubes.
6 oz. of onions cut into cubes.
1 bay leaf and 1 small sprig of thyme.
5 oz. of flour.

2 oz. of butter, ½ oz. of salt, 1 oz. of sugar, a pinch of pepper.
10 lbs. of raw tomatoes or 4 quarts canned.
2 quarts of white stock (10).

Preparation.—Fry the pork with the butter in a deep, thick-bottomed saucepan. When the pork is nearly melted, add the carrots, onions, and seasonings. Cook and stir the vegetables, then add the flour, which should be allowed to cook until it begins to brown. Now put in the tomatoes and white stock, mix the whole well, and set to boil on an open fire. At this point add the seasoning and a crushed clove of garlic, cover the saucepan, and place in a moderate oven, where it may cook for one and one-half hours. At the end of this time the sauce should be passed through a sieve, and it should boil while being stirred. Finally, pour it into a tureen, and butter its surface to avoid the formation of a skin.

Remarks.—A *purée* of tomatoes is also used in cookery; it is prepared in precisely the same fashion, except that the flour is omitted and only one pint of white stock is added.

30—HOLLANDAISE SAUCE   *Sauce Hollandaise*

Quantities Required for One Quart.—One and one-half lbs. of butter, the yolks of six eggs, one pinch of *mignonette* pepper and one-quarter oz. of salt, three tablespoons of good vinegar.

Preparation.—Put the salt, the *mignonette* pepper, the vinegar, and equal amount of water in a small saucepan, and reduce by three-quarters on the fire. Move the saucepan to a corner of the fire or into a double-boiler, and add a spoonful of cold water and the yolks. Beat with a whisk until the yolks thicken and have the consistency of cream. Then remove the pot to a tepid place and gradually pour the butter on the yolks while briskly stirring the sauce.

When the butter is absorbed, the sauce ought to be thick and firm. It is brought to the correct consistency with a little water, which also lightens it slightly, but the addition of water is optional. The sauce is completed by a drop of lemon juice, and it is rubbed through a fine sieve.

Remarks.—The consistency of sauces whose processes are identical with those of the Hollandaise may be varied at will; for instance, the number of yolks may be increased if a very thick sauce is desired, and it may be lessened in the reverse case. Also similar results may be obtained by cooking the eggs either more or less. As a rule, if a thick sauce be required, the yolks ought to be well cooked and the sauce kept almost cold in the making. Experience alone—the fruit of long practice—can teach the various devices which enable the skilled chef to obtain different results from the same kind and quality of material.

CHAPTER III

Remarks.—In order that the classification of the small sauces should be clear and methodical, I divide them into three parts.

The first part includes the small brown sauces; the second deals with the small white sauces and those suited to this part of the classification; while the third is concerned with the English sauces.

THE SMALL BROWN SAUCES

31—BIGARRADE SAUCE   *Sauce Bigarrade*

This sauce is principally used to accompany *braised* and *poëled* ducklings. In the first case, the duckling's *braising* stock, being thickened, constitutes a sauce. In the second case, the stock is clear, and the procedure in both cases is as follows:—

1. After having strained the *braising* sauce, completely remove its grease, and reduce it until it is very thick. Strain it once more through muslin, twisting it; then, in order to bring the sauce to its normal consistency, add the juice of six oranges and one lemon per quart of sauce. Finish with a small piece of lemon and orange rind cut regularly and finely, *Julienne*-fashion, and scalded for five minutes.

2. Strain the poëled stock, for ducklings or wild ducks, through linen; entirely remove the grease, and add four teaspoons of caramelized sugar (2344) dissolved in one tablespoon of vinegar per one-half point of stock, the juice of the oranges and the lemon and the *Julienne* of rinds, as for the braised-ducklings sauce indicated above.

32—BORDELAISE SAUCE   *Sauce Bordelaise*

Put into a saucepan two oz. of very finely minced shallots, one-half pint of good red wine, a pinch of *mignonette* pepper, and bits of thyme and bay leaf. Reduce the wine by three-quarters, and add one-half pint of half-*glaze* (23). Keep the sauce simmering for half

24

an hour; skin it from time to time, and strain it through linen or a sieve. When ready to serve, finish it with two tablespoons of dissolved meat glaze (15), a few drops of lemon-juice, and four oz. of beef-marrow, cut into slices or cubes and *poached* in slightly salted boiling water. This sauce may be buttered to the extent of about three oz. per pint, which makes it smoother, but less clear. It is especially suitable for grilled meat.

33—CHASSEUR SAUCE   *Sauce Chasseur*

Peel and mince six medium-sized mushrooms. Heat one-half oz. of butter and as much olive oil in a saucepan; put in the mushrooms, and fry the latter quickly until they are slightly browned. Now add a teaspoonful of minced shallots, and immediately remove half the butter; pour one-half pint of white wine and one glass of liqueur brandy into the saucepan; reduce this liquid to half, and finish the sauce with: one-half pint of half-glaze (23), one-quarter pint of tomato sauce (29), and one tablespoon of meat-glaze (15). Set to boil for five minutes more, and complete with a teaspoon of chopped parsley.

34—BROWN CHAUD-FROID SAUCE   *Sauce Chaud-Froid Brune*

Put one quart of half-glaze (23) into a saucepan with one-fifth pint of truffle *essence*. Put the pan on an open fire, and reduce its contents; while making same add to the sauce, in small quantities at a time, one and one-half pints of aspic.

The degree of reduction in this sauce is a good third, but, to be quite certain, a test of its consistency may be made by allowing it to cool a little. After the reduction, carefully taste, and rectify the seasoning if necessary; mix a little Madeira or Port with the sauce, away from the fire, and strain through muslin or, preferably, through the finest possible sieve. Stir the sauce now and then while it cools, until it is sufficiently liquid, and at the same time consistent enough, to coat a spoon evenly with a film. Its use will be explained among the recipes of the different kinds of Chaud-froids.

35—VARIETIES OF THE CHAUD-FROID SAUCE
Diverses Sauces Chaud-Froid

For Ducks.—Prepare the sauce as for (34), adding to it (for the prescribed quantity) one-half pint of duck *fumet* obtained from the skeletons and remains of roast duckling, and finish it, away from the fire, with the juice of four oranges and a heaped tablespoon of orange rind, cut finely, *Julienne*-fashion, and scalded for five minutes.

For Game Birds.—Treat the Chaud-Froid sauce as indicated in 34, adding one-half pint of the *fumet* of the game constituting the dish in order to lend it that game's characteristic taste. Observe the same precaution for the cooling.

For Fish.—Proceed as in (34), but substitute the Espagnole of fish (22) for the half glaze; intensify the first Espagnole with one-half pint of very clear fish *essence;* use *Lenten* jelly instead of meat jelly.

Remarks upon the Use of Chaud-Froid Sauces.—The chaud-froid sauce may be prepared beforehand, and when it is wanted it need only be gently melted without heating it too much. It ought simply to be made sufficiently liquid to give a good coating to substances immersed in it.

36—DEVILLED SAUCE   *Sauce Diable*

Put in a saucepan two oz. of sliced shallots and one-third pint of white wine. Reduce the latter to two-thirds, add one-half pint of half-glaze (23), reduce to two-thirds again, season strongly with cayenne pepper, and strain through muslin. This sauce may be served with grilled fowls or pigeons. It also forms an excellent accompaniment to left-over meat which needs a spicy sauce.

37—ESCOFFIER DEVILLED SAUCE   *Sauce Diable Escoffier*

This sauce, which may be bought ready-made, is admirably fitted to accompany grilled fish and grills in general. In order to make it ready, all that is needed is to add an equal amount of fresh butter to it, the latter being previously well softened so as to ensure its perfect mixture with the sauce.

38—GENEVOISE SAUCE   *Sauce Genevoise*

Heat two oz. of butter in a saucepan; add one lb. of *Mirepoix* (228) without bacon. Slightly brown, add two lbs. of head of salmon and trimmings or bones of fish, and cook with lid on for twenty minutes. Let the saucepan lean slightly to one side, so that the butter may be drained; moisten with one bottle of excellent red wine; reduce the latter by half; add one pint of *Lenten* Espagnole (24), and allow to cook gently for half an hour.

Rub the sauce through a sieve, pressing it so as to extract all the *essence.* Let it rest awhile; carefully remove the fat which has risen to the surface, and add one liqueur-glass of burnt brandy, one-half pint of red wine, and as much fish *fumet*. Boil again, then move saucepan to the side of fire and skim for one and one-half hours. Frequently remove what the boiling causes to rise to the surface, this second period of cooking being only to ensure the purification of the sauce. If the boiling has been properly handled, the sauce should reach the proper degree of reduction and can be skimmed at the same time. It is then strained through muslin or a fine sieve, and it is finished at the last minute with a few drops of anchovy *essence* and four oz. of butter per quart of sauce.

N.B.—The Genevoise Sauce, like all red-wine sauces, may be served without being buttered. It is thus clearer and more pleasing in color, but the addition of butter in small quantities makes it mellower and more palatable.

38a—REMARKS ON RED WINE SAUCES
Reflexions sur des Sauces au Vin Rouge

In the general repertory of cooking we also have, in the way of red-wine sauces, the "Bourguignonne," "Matelote," and "Red-Wine" sauces, which are closely allied to the "Genevoise," and only differ from it in details of procedure.

The "Bourguignonne" Sauce is composed of red-wine accompanied by seasonings, and reduced by half. In accordance with ordinary principles, it is thickened by means of three oz. of *manié* butter per quart of reduced wine. This sauce is buttered with four oz. of butter per quart, and is especially regarded as a domestic preparation for *poached,* moulded, and hard-boiled eggs.

"Matelote" Sauce is made from Court-bouillon (166) with red wine which has been used for cooking fish. This Court-bouillon, with the mushroom peelings added, is reduced by two-thirds, and is thickened with one pint of *Lenten* Espagnole (24) per pint of the reduced Court-bouillon.

This sauce should be reduced by a third, strained through a fine sieve, and finished by means of two oz. of butter and a little cayenne per pint of sauce.

The Red-Wine Sauce resembles the two preceding ones in so far as it contains *Mirepoix* browned in butter and diluted with red wine. The wine is reduced by half, thickened by a pint of *Lenten* Espagnole per pint of the reduction, and the sauce is skimmed for about twenty minutes. It is strained through a fine sieve, and finished, when ready, by a few drops of anchovy *essence,* a little cayenne, and two oz. of butter per pint of sauce.

39—GRAND-VENEUR SAUCE — *Sauce Grand-Veneur*

Take one pint of Poivrade Sauce (49) and boil it, adding one pint of game stock (5) to keep it light; reduce the sauce by a good third; remove it from the fire, and add four tablespoons of red-currant jelly. When the latter is well dissolved, complete the sauce by adding one-quarter pint of cream per pint of sauce.

This sauce is the proper accompaniment for joints of venison.

40—ITALIAN SAUCE — *Sauce Italienne*

Ordinary Italian Sauce.—Put into a saucepan six tablespoons of Duxelles (223), two oz. of very lean, cooked ham, cut very finely, *brunoise*-fashion, and one pint of half-glaze (23) tomato. Boil for ten minutes, and complete, at the moment of serving, with one teaspoon of parsley, chervil, and tarragon, minced and mixed.

Lenten Italian Sauce.—Same preparation, only omit the ham, and substitute *Lent* Espagnole (24) (combined with fish *fumet* made from the fish for which the sauce is intended) for half-glaze (23) with tomatoes.

41—THICKENED GRAVY — *Jus Lié*

Boil one pint of poultry or veal stock (10) (according to the nature of the dish the gravy is intended for). Thicken this sauce by means of three-quarters oz. of *fecula* (cornstarch, etc.), diluted with a little cold water or gravy, and pour this binding into the boiling gravy, being careful to stir briskly.

The thickened gravy with the veal-stock (10) base is used for choicest cuts of butcher's meat; the same gravy with a poultry-stock base is for breasts of poultry.

42—TOMATOED VEAL GRAVY — *Jus Lié Tomaté*

Add to one pint of veal stock (10) two oz. of *purée* and one-quarter pint of tomato juice, and reduce by a fifth. Strain the gravy through linen. This gravy is used for various meat.

43—LYONNAISE SAUCE — *Sauce Lyonnaise*

Finely mince two oz. of onions and brown them slightly in two oz. of butter. Moisten with one-quarter pint of white wine and as much vinegar; reduce the liquid; add one and one-half pints of clear half-glaze (23), and set to cook slowly for half an hour. Rub the sauce through a fine sieve.

N.B.—The onion may be left in the sauce or not, according to the preparation for which it is intended and to suit the taste.

44—MADEIRA SAUCE *Sauce Madère*

Put one and one-half pints of half-glaze (23) into a saucepan, and reduce it on a brisk fire to a stiff consistency. When it reaches this point, take it off the fire and add one-fifth pint of Madeira to it, which brings it back to its normal consistency. Strain through a fine sieve, and keep it warm without allowing it to boil.

45—MARROW SAUCE *Sauce Moelle*

Follow the proportions as indicated under "Sauce Bordelaise" (32) for the necessary quantity of this sauce, the Marrow Sauce being only a variety of the Bordelaise. Finish it with six oz. per quart of beef marrow, cut into cubes, *poached* and well drained, and one teaspoon of chopped parsley, scalded for a second. If the sauce is to accompany vegetables, finish it, away from the fire, with three oz. of butter, and then add the cubes of marrow and the parsley.

46—PINE-NUT SAUCE *Sauce Pignons*

Take the necessary amount of Poivrade Sauce (49), and let it boil. Now, for one pint of sauce, prepare an infusion of juniper berries, with one-quarter pint of water and two oz. of coarsely chopped berries; one oz. of toasted pine-nuts, and one oz. of raisins, seeded and washed, and left to soak in tepid water for about an hour. Finish the sauce, when serving, by adding the infusion of juniper berries strained through linen, the toasted pine-nuts, the soaked raisins, and one-eighth pint of Madeira wine.

This sauce is specially suited to joints of venison.

47—PERIGUEUX SAUCE *Sauce Perigueux*

Prepare a "Sauce Madère" (44), and add to the half-glaze (23), to be reduced, half its volume of very strong veal stock (10), and keep it a little thicker than usual. Finish this sauce by adding one-sixth pint of truffle *essence* and three oz. of chopped truffles per quart of Madeira Sauce (44). It is used for numerous small entrées, timbales, hot pâtés, etc.

48—PIQUANTE SAUCE *Sauce Piquante*

Put into a saucepan two oz. of minced shallots, one-quarter pint of vinegar, and as much white wine. Reduce the liquid by a good half, and add one pint of half-glaze (23); set the sauce to boil, and skim it for half an hour. At the last moment finish it, away from the fire, with two oz. of gherkins, one oz. of capers, and a teaspoon of chervil, parsley, and tarragon, mixed; all the ingredients to be finely chopped. This sauce generally accompanies grilled or boiled pork, and cold left-over meat minced, which needs spicy flavoring.

49—ORDINARY POIVRADE SAUCE   *Sauce Poivrade Ordinaire*

1. Heat two oz. of butter in a saucepan, and add one lb. of raw *Mirepoix* (228). Fry the vegetables until they are well browned; moisten with one-quarter pint of vinegar and one-half pint of *Marinade* (169); reduce to two-thirds; add one pint of Espagnole Sauce (22), and cook for three-quarters of an hour. Ten minutes before straining the sauce, put in a few crushed peppercorns. If the pepper were put in the sauce earlier, it might make it bitter.

2. Strain the sauce through a sieve, pressing the seasonings; add a further one-half pint of *Marinade,* and skim for one-quarter of an hour, keeping it simmering the while. Strain again through a fine sieve, and finish the sauce, when ready for serving, with two oz. of butter.

This sauce is suitable for joints marinated or not.

50—POIVRADE SAUCE FOR VENISON   *Sauce Poivrade pour Gibier*

Fry, with two oz. of butter and two oz. of oil, one lb. of raw *Mirepoix* (228) to which are added four lbs. of well-broken bones and ground-game trimmings. When the whole is well browned, drain off the grease, and dilute with one pint of vinegar and one pint of white wine. Reduce this liquid by three-quarters, then add three quarts of game stock and a quart of Espagnole Sauce (22). Boil, cover the saucepan, and put into a moderate oven, where it should stay for at least three hours. At the end of this time take out the saucepan and pour its contents through a fine sieve placed over a tureen; press the remains so as to expel all the sauce they hold, and pour the sauce into a tall, thick saucepan. Add enough game stock (8) and *Marinade,* mixed in equal parts, to produce three quarts in all of sauce, and gently reduce the latter while skimming it. As it diminishes in volume, it should be passed through muslin into smaller saucepans, and the reduction should be stopped when only a quart of sauce remains.

N.B.—This sauce, like red-wine sauces, may be served as it stands. It is brilliant, clear, and perhaps more pleasing, but the addition of a certain quantity of butter (four oz. per quart) makes it perfectly mellow, and admirably completes its fragrance.

51—PROVENCALE SAUCE   *Sauce Provençale*

Peel, remove the seeds, press and coarsely chop twelve medium tomatoes. Heat in a saucepan one-fifth pint of oil, until it begins to smoke a little; add the tomatoes seasoned with pepper and salt; add a crushed garlic clove, a pinch of powdered sugar, one teaspoon of chopped parsley, and allow to cook gently for half an hour. In reality, true Provençale is nothing but a fine *fondue* of tomatoes with garlic.

52—ROBERT SAUCE   *Sauce Robert*

Finely mince a large onion and put it into a saucepan with butter. Fry the onion gently and without letting it brown. Dilute with one-third pint of white wine, reduce the latter by one-third, add one pint of half-glaze (23), and leave to simmer for twenty minutes. When serving, finish the sauce with one tablespoon of meat glaze (15), one teaspoon of dry mustard, and one pinch of powdered sugar. If, when finished, the sauce has to wait, it should be kept warm in a double-boiler, as it must not boil again. This sauce—of a spicy flavor—is best suited to grilled and boiled pork. It may also be used for a mince of the same meat.

53—ROBERT SAUCE ESCOFFIER   *Sauce Robert Escoffier*

This sauce may be bought ready-made. It is used either hot or cold. It is especially suitable for pork, veal, poultry, and even fish, and is generally used hot with grills after the equal quantity of excellent brown stock (7) has been added to it. It may also be served cold to accompany cold meat.

54—ROUENNAISE SAUCE   *Sauce Rouennaise*

Prepare a "Bordelaise" sauce (32). The diluting liquid of this sauce must be an excellent red wine. For one pint of sauce, pass four raw ducks' livers through a sieve; add the resulting *purée* to the Bordelaise, and heat the latter for a few minutes in order to *poach* the liver. Be careful, however, not to heat the sauce too much nor too long, lest the liver be cooked. Serve this sauce with duckling à la Rouennaise (1754).

55—SALMIS SAUCE   *Sauce Salmis*

The base of this sauce, which rather resembles the *cullis,* is unchangeable. Its diluting liquid only changes according to the kind of birds or game to be treated, and whether this game is to be considered ordinary or *Lenten.*

Cut and gently brown in butter five oz. of *Mirepoix* (228). Add
the skin detached from the limbs and the chopped skeleton of the
bird being used, and moisten with one pint of white wine. Reduce
the latter to two-thirds, add one-half pint of half-glaze (23), and
boil gently for three-quarters of an hour. Pass through a strainer,
while pressing down the bird and the seasonings, with the view of
extracting their *essence*, and thin the *cullis* thus obtained by means
of one-half pint of game stock (5) or mushroom liquor, if the game
be *Lenten*. Now skim for about one hour, finally reduce the sauce,
bring it to its proper consistency with a little mushroom liquor and
truffle *essence*, rub it through a fine sieve, and butter it slightly at
the last moment.

56—TURTLE SAUCE   *Sauce Tortue*

Boil one-half pint of veal stock (9), adding a small sprig of sage,
sweet marjoram, rosemary, basil, thyme, and as much bay leaf, two
oz. of mushroom peelings, and one oz. of parsley. Cover and allow
to steep for half an hour. Two minutes before straining the infusion, add four coarsely chopped peppercorns.

After straining through fine linen, add one-half pint of half-glaze
(23) and as much tomato sauce (29) (away from the fire) with four
tablespoons of sherry, a little truffle (29) *essence*, and a good pinch
of cayenne.

N.B.—As this sauce must be spicy, the use of cayenne suggests
itself, but great caution should be observed, as there must be no
excess of this condiment.

57—VENISON SAUCE   *Sauce Venaison*

Prepare a Poivrade sauce (50) for game. Finish this sauce with
two tablespoons of red-currant jelly, previously dissolved, and
mixed with five tablespoons of fresh cream per pint of sauce. This
addition of cream and red-currants must be made away from the
fire.

Serve this sauce with large-game.

Small White and Compound Sauces

58—AMERICAN SAUCE   *Sauce Americaine*

This sauce is that of lobster prepared "à l'Américaine" (939). As
it generally accompanies a fish, the meat of the lobster or lobsters
which have served in its preparation is sliced and used as the garnish
of the fish.

59—ANCHOVY SAUCE   *Sauce Anchois*

Put into a small saucepan one pint of unbuttered "Normande Sauce" (99), and finish it, away from the fire, with three oz. of anchovy butter (281), and one oz. of anchovy fillets, washed, dried, and cut into small pieces.

60—AURORE SAUCE   *Sauce Aurore*

Into one-half pint of boiling velouté (25) put the same quantity of very red tomato *purée* (29), and mix the two. Let the sauce boil a little, pass it through a fine sieve, and finish, away from the fire, with three oz. of butter.

61—LENTEN AURORE SAUCE   *Sauce Aurore Maigre*

This sauce is made like the preceding one, with the same quantities of velouté and tomato *purée,* replacing ordinary velouté by fish velouté (26a).

62—BEARNAISE SAUCE   *Sauce Béarnaise*

Put into a small saucepan one teaspoon of chopped shallots, two oz. of chopped tarragon stalks, three oz. of chervil, some *mignonette* pepper, a pinch of salt, and four tablespoons of vinegar. Reduce the vinegar by two-thirds, take off the fire, let the pan cool a little, and add to this reduction the yolks of five eggs. Now put the saucepan on a low fire and gradually combine with the yolks six oz. of melted butter. Whisk the sauce briskly, to ensure the cooking of the yolks, which alone, by gradual cooking, effect the thickening of the sauce.

When the butter is combined with the sauce, rub it through a fine sieve, and finish it with a teaspoon of chervil and chopped tarragon leaves. Complete the seasoning with a pinch of cayenne. This sauce should not be served very hot, as it is really a mayonnaise with butter. It need only be tepid, for it would probably curdle if it were over-heated. Serve it with grilled meat or poultry.

63—BEARNAISE SAUCE WITH MEAT GLAZE, CALLED VALOIS
**   SAUCE OR FOYOT SAUCE**
        Sauce Béarnaise à la Glace de Viande, dite Valois ou Foyot

Prepare a Béarnaise sauce as explained in (62). Complete it with three tablespoons of dissolved pale meat glaze (15), which may be added in small quantities at a time. Serve it with various meats.

64—TOMATOED BEARNAISE SAUCE OR CHORON SAUCE

Sauce Béarnaise Tomatée ou Sauce Choron

Proceed in exactly the same way as for Béarnaise (62). When the sauce is made and rubbed through a fine sieve, finish it with one-third pint of very red tomato *purée*. In this case the final addition of chervil and tarragon should not be made.

This is proper to "Tournedos Choron," but it may accompany grilled poultry and veal or pork.

65—BERCY SAUCE
Sauce Bercy

Heat two oz. of chopped shallots. Moisten with one-half pint of white wine and as much fish *fumet,* or, when possible, the same quantity of fish liquor, the latter being, of course, that of a fish similar to the one the sauce is to accompany. Reduce to a good third, add one-third pint of velouté (25), let the sauce boil some time, and finish it, away from the fire, with four oz. of butter (added by degrees), a few drops of fish *glaze,* half the juice of a lemon, and one oz. of chopped parsley.

Serve with medium-sized *poached* fish.

66—BUTTER SAUCE
Sauce au Beurre

Mix two oz. of sifted flour with two oz. of melted butter. Dilute with one quart of boiling water, salted to the extent of one-quarter oz. per quart. Stir briskly to ensure a perfect blending, and do not allow to boil. Add immediately the yolks of six eggs mixed with one-quarter pint of cream and the juice of half a lemon. Rub through a fine sieve, and finish the sauce with five oz. of best fresh butter.

Be careful that the sauce does not boil after it has been thickened.

67—BONNEFOY SAUCE, OR WHITE BORDELAISE SAUCE
Sauce Bonnefoy, ou Sauce Bordelaise Blanche

Put in a saucepan two oz. of minced shallots and one-half pint of Graves, Sauterne, or any other excellent white Bordeaux. Reduce the wine almost entirely, add one-quarter pint of velouté (25), let it simmer twenty minutes, and rub it through a fine sieve. Finish it, away from the fire, with six oz. of butter and a little chopped tarragon.

Serve it with grilled fish or grilled white meat.

68—CAPER SAUCE *Sauce aux Capres*

This is a derivative of the Butter Sauce (66), and there need only be added two tablespoons of capers per pint of sauce. It frequently accompanies boiled fish of all kinds.

69—CARDINAL SAUCE *Sauce Cardinal*

Boil one pint of Béchamel (28), to which add one-half pint of fish *fumet* and a little truffle *essence,* and reduce by a quarter. Finish the sauce, when serving, with three tablespoons of cream and three oz. of very red lobster butter (149).

70—MUSHROOM SAUCE *Sauce aux Champignons*

If this be intended for poultry, add one-fifth pint of mushroom liquor and eight oz. of button-mushroom caps turned or grooved and cooked, to one pint of very stiff Allemande Sauce (27).

If it be intended for fish, take one pint of fish velouté (26a) thickened with the yolks of four eggs, and finish it with mushroom liquor, as above.

The sauce that I suggest for poultry may also be used for fish, after adding the necessary quantity of fish *fumet.*

71—CHÂTEAUBRIAND SAUCE *Sauce Châteaubriand*

Put one oz. of chopped shallots, a sprig of thyme and a bit of bay leaf, one oz. of mushroom peelings, and one-quarter pint of white wine into a saucepan. Reduce the wine almost entirely, add one-half pint of veal gravy, and reduce again until the liquid only measures one-quarter pint. Strain through muslin, and finish the sauce away from the fire with four oz. of butter "Maître d'Hotel" (150), to which may be added a little chopped tarragon. Serve with grilled fillet of beef, otherwise "Châteaubriand."

72—WHITE CHAUD-FROID SAUCE *Sauce Chaud-Froid Blanche*

Boil one pint of velouté (25) in a saucepan, and add three-quarters pint of melted white poultry aspic (159). Put the saucepan on an open fire, reduce the sauce by a third, stirring constantly, and gradually add one-half pint of very fresh cream. When the sauce has reached the desired degree of consistency rub it through a fine sieve, and stir it frequently while it cools, for fear of a skin forming on its surface, for if this happened it would have to be strained again. When serving, this sauce should be cold, so that it may properly coat a spoon and yet be liquid enough to permit the latter being easily dipped into it.

73—ORDINARY CHAUD-FROID SAUCE   *Sauce Chaud-Froid Ordinaire*

Proceed exactly as above, substituting Allemande Sauce (27) for the velouté, and reducing the quantity of cream to one-quarter pint. Observe the same precautions while cooling.

74—CHAUD-FROID SAUCE, A L'AURORE

Sauce Chaud-Froid à l'Aurore

Prepare a white Chaud-Froid (72). The same may be colored by the addition of fine red tomato *purée* (29)—more or less to match the desired shade—or by an infusion of paprika, according to the use for which it is intended. This last product is preferable when not too deep a shade is required.

75—CHAUD-FROID SAUCE VERT-PRE

Sauce Chaud-Froid, au Vert-Pré

Add to the velouté (25) of the white Chaud-Froid (72) sauce, at the same time as the jelly aspic, an infusion prepared thus:—Boil one-quarter pint of white wine, and add to it one pinch of chervil stalks, a similar quantity of tarragon leaves, chives, and parsley leaves. Cover, allow infusion to proceed away from the fire for ten minutes, and strain through linen.

Treat the sauce as explained, and finish with spinach-green (143). The shade of the sauce must not be too pronounced, but must remain a pale green. The coloring principle must therefore be added with caution and in small quantities, until the correct shade is obtained. Use this sauce for Chaud-Froids of fowl, particularly that kind distinguished as *"Printanier."*

76—LENT CHAUD-FROID SAUCE   *Sauce Chaud-Froid Maigre*

Proceed as for white Chaud-Froid (22), using the same quantities, and taking note of the following modifications:—

1. Substitute fish velouté (26a) for ordinary velouté.
2. Substitute white fish jelly for poultry aspic.

Remarks.—I have adopted the use of this ordinary Chaud-Froid sauce for the glazing of fillets and scallops of fish and shell-fish, instead of cleared Mayonnaise, formerly used, which had certain inconveniences—not the least being the oozing out of the oil under the shrinkage of the gelatine. This difficulty does not obtain in the ordinary Chaud-Froid. the definite and pronounced flavor of which is better than that of the cleared Mayonnaise.

77—CHERRY SAUCE ESCOFFIER   *Sauce aux Cerises Escoffier*

This sauce may be bought ready-made. Like the Robert Sauce, it can be served hot or cold. It is an excellent addition to venison, and even to small ground-game. Saddle of venison with this sauce constitutes one of the greatest delicacies that an epicure could desire.

78—CHIVRY SAUCE   *Sauce Chivry*

In one-half pint of boiling poultry stock (10) put a large pinch of chervil *pluches,* tarragon and parsley leaves, a head of young pimpernel (the qualification here is very important, for this aromatic plant grows bitter as it matures), and a good pinch of chives. Cover, and let infusion proceed for ten to twelve minutes; then add the liquid (strained through linen) to one pint of velouté (25). Boil, reduce by a quarter, and complete it with two oz. of Green Butter (143). Chivry Sauce is admirably suited to boiled or *poached* poultry.

79—CREAM SAUCE   *Sauce à la Crème*

Boil one pint of Béchamel Sauce (28), and add one-quarter pint of cream to it. Reduce on an open fire until the sauce has become very thick; then strain through a fine sieve. Bring to its normal degree of consistency by gradually adding, away from the fire, one-quarter pint of very fresh cream and a few drops of lemon-juice. Serve this sauce with boiled fish, poultry, eggs, and various vegetables.

80—SHRIMP SAUCE   *Sauce aux Crevettes*

Boil one pint of fish velouté (26a) or, failing this, Béchamel sauce (28), and add to it one-quarter pint of cream and one-quarter pint of very clear fish *fumet.* Reduce to one pint, and finish the sauce, away from the fire, with two oz. of Shrimp Butter (145) and two oz. of shelled shrimps' tails.

81—CURRY SAUCE   *Sauce Currie*

Slightly brown the following vegetables in butter:—Twelve oz. of minced onions, one oz. of parsley roots, four oz. of minced celery, a small sprig of thyme, a bit of bay leaf, and a little mace. Sprinkle with two oz. of flour and a teaspoon of curry powder. Cook the flour for some minutes without letting it brown, and dilute with one and one-half pints of white stock (10). Boil, cook gently for three-quarters of an hour, and rub through a fine sieve. Now beat the sauce, remove its grease, and keep it in a double-boiler. Serve this sauce with fish, shell-fish, poultry, and various egg-preparations.

N.B.—This sauce is sometimes flavored with cocoa-nut water or milk in the proportion of one-quarter of the liquid.

82—DIPLOMATE SAUCE   *Sauce Diplomate*

Take one pint of Normande Sauce (99), and finish it with two oz. of lobster butter (149) and three tablespoons of lobster meat, and truffles cut into small, regular cubes.

83—HERB SAUCE   *Sauce aux Fines Herbes*

Prepare one pint of white-wine sauce (111). Finish it away from the fire with three oz. of shallot butter (146), a tablespoon of parsley, chervil, tarragon, and chives, chopped and mixed. Serve this sauce with boiled or *poached* fish.

84—GOOSEBERRY SAUCE   *Sauce aux Groseilles*

Prepare one pint of butter sauce (66). Meanwhile put one lb. of green gooseberries into a small copper saucepan containing boiling water. Boil for five minutes, then drain the gooseberries, and put them in a little saucepan with one-half pint of white wine and three oz. of powdered sugar. Gently cook the gooseberries, rub them through a fine sieve, and add the pulp to the butter sauce. This sauce is excellent with grilled mackerel and the *poached* fillets of that fish.

85—HUNGARIAN SAUCE   *Sauce Hongroise*

Gently fry in butter, without browning, two tablespoons of chopped onions seasoned with table-salt and half a teaspoon of paprika. Moisten with one-quarter pint of white wine, add a small herb bunch, reduce the wine by two-thirds, and remove the herbs.

Finish with one pint of ordinary or *Lenten* Velouté (26a), according to the use for which the sauce is intended, and boil moderately for five minutes. Then rub the sauce through a fine sieve, and complete it with two oz. of butter. Remember this sauce should be of a tender, pink shade, which it must owe to the paprika alone.

It forms an ideal accompaniment to choice morsels of lamb and veal, eggs, poultry, and fish.

86—OYSTER SAUCE   *Sauce aux Huîtres*

Take one pint of Normande Sauce (99), finish it as directed in that recipe, and complete it with one-quarter pint of reduced oyster liquor, strained through linen, and twelve *poached* and trimmed oysters.

87—IVORY SAUCE, OR ALBUFERA SAUCE *Sauce Albufera*

Take the necessary quantity of Suprême Sauce (106a). Add to this four tablespoons of dissolved, pale, meat glaze (15) per quart of sauce, in order to lend the latter that ivory-white tint which characterizes it. Serve this sauce chiefly with poultry and *poached* sweetbread.

88—JOINVILLE SAUCE *Sauce Joinville*

Prepare one pint of Normande Sauce (99), as given in the first part of the recipe, and complete it with two oz. of shrimp butter (45) and two oz. of crayfish butter (147). If this sauce is to accompany a fish à la Joinville, which includes a special garnish, it is served as it stands. If it is served with a large, boiled, ungarnished fish, one oz. of very black truffles cut *Julienne*-fashion should be added. As may be seen, Joinville Sauce differs from similar preparations in the final operation where crayfish and shrimp butter are combined.

89—MALTESE SAUCE *Sauce Maltaise*

To the Hollandaise Sauce (30), add, when serving up, the juice of two blood oranges (these late-season oranges being especially suitable for this sauce) and half a teaspoonful of grated orange-rind.

Maltese Sauce is the finest for asparagus.

90—MARINIERE SAUCE *Sauce Marinière*

Take the necessary quantity of Bercy Sauce (65), and add, per pint of sauce, one-quarter pint of mussel liquor and a binding composed of the yolks of three eggs.

Serve this with small *poached* fish and more particularly with mussels.

91—MORNAY SAUCE *Sauce Mornay*

Boil one pint of Béchamel Sauce (28) with one-quarter pint of the *fumet* of the fish, poultry, or vegetable, which is to constitute the dish. Reduce by a good quarter, and add two oz. of Gruyère and two oz. of grated Parmesan.

Put the sauce on the fire again for a few minutes, and ensure the melting of the cheese by stirring with a small whisk. Finish the sauce away from the fire with two oz. of butter added by degrees.

92—MOUSSELINE SAUCE   *Sauce Mousseline*

To a Hollandaise Sauce (30), add, just before serving up, one-half pint of stiffly-whipped cream per pint of sauce.

93—MOUSSEUSE SAUCE   *Sauce Mousseuse*

Scald and wipe a small pan, and put into it one-half lb. of stiff *manié* butter, properly softened. Season this butter with table-salt and a few drops of lemon-juice, and whisk it while gradually adding one-third pint of cold water. Finish with two tablespoons of very firm, whipped cream. This preparation, though classified as a sauce, is really a compound butter, which is served with boiled fish. The heat of the fish is sufficient to melt it, and its appearance is infinitely more agreeable than that of plain, melted butter.

94—MUSTARD SAUCE   *Sauce Moutarde*

Take the necessary quantity of butter sauce and complete it, away from the fire, with one tablespoon of mustard per pint of sauce.

N.B.—If the sauce has to wait, it must be kept in a double-boiler, for it should not on any account boil. It is served with certain small grilled fish, especially fresh herrings.

95—NANTUA SAUCE   *Sauce Nantua*

Boil one pint of Béchamel Sauce (28), add one-half pint of cream, and reduce by a third. Rub it through a fine sieve, and finish it with a further addition of two tablespoons of cream, three oz. of very fine crayfish butter (147), and one tablespoon of small, shelled crayfishes' tails.

96—NEWBURG SAUCE   *Sauce Newburg*

First Method (with Raw Lobsters).—Divide a two lb. lobster into four parts. Remove its creamy parts, chop them finely with two oz. of butter, and put them aside.

Heat in a saucepan one and one-half oz. of butter and as much oil, and add the pieces of lobster, well seasoned with salt and cayenne. Fry until the pieces assume a fine, red color; entirely drain away the butter, and add two tablespoons of burnt brandy and one-third pint of Marsala or old Sherry.

Reduce the wine by two-thirds, and douse the lobster with one-third pint of cream and one-half pint of fish *fumet*. Now add a herb bunch, cover the saucepan, and gently cook for twenty-five minutes. Then drain the lobster in a sieve, remove the meat and cut it into cubes, and finish the sauce by adding the creamy portions put aside from the first. Boil so as to ensure the cooking of these latter portions; add the meat, cut into cubes, and test for the seasoning.

N.B.—The addition of the meat to the sauce is optional; instead of cutting it into cubes it may be cooked and arranged on the fish constituting the dish.

97—NEWBURG SAUCE WITH COOKED LOBSTER
Sauce Newburg avec Homard Cuit

The lobster having been cooked in a *Court-bouillon* (166), shell the tail and slice it up. Arrange these slices in a saucepan liberally buttered; season them strongly with salt and cayenne, and heat them on both sides so as to effect the reddening of the skin. Immerse, to cover, in a good Sherry, and almost entirely reduce same.

When serving, pour on the slices a binding mixture composed of one-third pint of fresh cream and the yolks of two eggs. Gently stir, away from the fire, and roll the saucepan about until the blending is completed.

Originally, these two sauces, like the American, were exclusively composed of, and served with, lobster. They were one with the two very excellent preparations of lobster which bear their name. In its two forms lobster may only be served at lunch, many people with delicate stomachs being unable to digest it at night. To obviate this serious difficulty, I have made it a practice to serve lobster sauce with fillets or Mousselines of sole, adding the lobster as a garnish only. And this innovation proved most welcome to the public.

By using such condiments as curry and paprika, excellent varieties of this sauce may be obtained, which are particularly suited to sole and other white *Lenten* fish. In either of these cases it is well to add a little rice "à l'Indienne" (2254) to the fish.

98—NOISETTE SAUCE   *Sauce Noisette*
Prepare a Hollandaise Sauce (30). Add two oz. of hazel-nut butter (155) at the last moment.

Serve this with salmon, trout, and all boiled fish in general.

99—NORMANDY SAUCE   *Sauce Normandie*
Put in a saucepan one pint of fish velouté (26a), three tablespoons of mushroom liquor, as much oyster liquor, and twice as much sole *fumet* (11), the yolks of three eggs, a few drops of lemon-juice,

and one-quarter pint of cream. Reduce by a good third over an open fire, season with a little cayenne, rub through a fine sieve, and finish with two oz. of butter and four tablespoons of good cream.

This sauce is proper to fillet of sole "à la Normande" (856), but it is also frequently used as the base of other small sauces.

100—ORIENTAL SAUCE   *Sauce Orientale*

Take one pint of American sauce (58), season with curry, and reduce to a third. Then add, away from the fire, one-quarter pint of cream per pint of sauce.

Serve this sauce in the same way as American Sauce.

101—POULETTE SAUCE   *Sauce Poulette*

Boil for a few minutes one pint of Sauce Allemande (27), and add six tablespoons of mushroom liquor. Finish, away from the fire, with two oz. of butter, a few drops of lemon-juice, and one teaspoonful of chopped parsley. Use this sauce with certain vegetables, but more generally with sheep's shanks.

102—RAVIGOTE SAUCE   *Sauce Ravigote*

Reduce by half, one-quarter pint of white wine with half as much vinegar. Add one pint of ordinary velouté (25), boil gently for a few minutes, and finish with one and one-half oz. of shallot butter (146) and one teaspoon of chervil, tarragon, and chopped chives. This sauce accompanies boiled poultry (1444) and certain white *"abats"* (lights of veal, pork, and lamb).

103—REGENCY SAUCE   *Sauce Régence*

If this sauce is to garnish poultry, boil one pint of Allemande Sauce (27) with six tablespoons of mushroom *essence* and two table-spoons of truffle *essence*. Finish with four tablespoons of poultry *glaze* (16).

If it is to garnish fish, substitute for the Allemande Sauce (27) some fish velouté (26a) thickened with egg-yolks and the *essences* of mushroom and truffle. Complete with some fish *essence*.

104—SOUBISE SAUCE   *Sauce Soubise*

Cook in butter two lbs. of finely-minced onions, scalded for three minutes and well dried. This cooking of the onions in butter increases their flavor. Now add one-half pint of thickened Béchamel (28); season with salt and a teaspoon of powdered sugar. Cook gently for half an hour, rub through a fine sieve, and complete the sauce with some tablespoons of cream and two oz. of butter.

105—SOUBISE SAUCE WITH RICE   *Sauce Soubise au Riz*

The same quantity as above of minced onions, scalded and well drained. Garnish the bottom and the sides of a tall, medium saucepan with some thin slices of fat bacon. Add the onions, together with one-quarter lb. of Carolina or Southern rice, one pint of white consommé, a large pinch of powdered sugar, and the necessary salt. Cook gently in the front of the oven for three-quarters of an hour. Then put the onions and rice through a grinder, rub the resulting *purée* through a fine sieve, and finish with cream and butter as in the preceding case.

N.B.—This sauce, being more consistent than the former, is used as a garnish just as often as a sauce.

106—TOMATOED SOUBISE SAUCE   *Sauce Soubise Tomatée*

Prepare a Soubise in accordance with the first of the two above recipes, and add to it one-third of its volume of very red tomato *purée* (29).

REMARKS

1. The Soubise is rather a *cullis* than a sauce, and its consistency must be greater than that of a sauce.

2. The addition of Béchamel (28) in Soubise is preferable to that of rice, since it makes it smoother. If, in certain cases, rice is used as a binding element, it is to give the Soubise more consistency.

3. In accordance with the uses to which it may be put, the Tomato Soubise may be finally seasoned either with curry or paprika.

106a—SUPREME SAUCE   *Sauce Suprême*

The salient characteristics of Suprême Sauce are its perfect whiteness and delicacy. It is generally prepared in small quantities only.

Preparation.—Put one and one-half pints of very clear poultry stock (10) and one-quarter pint of mushroom cooking liquor into a saucepan. Reduce to two-thirds; add one pint of "poultry velouté" (26); reduce on an open fire, stirring with the spatula, and combine one-half pint of excellent cream with the sauce, this last ingredient being added little by little.

When the sauce has reached the desired consistency, strain it through a sieve, and add another one-quarter pint of cream and two oz. of best butter. Stir with a spoon, from time to time, or keep the pan well covered.

107—VENETIAN SAUCE   *Sauce Venitienne*

Put into a saucepan one tablespoon of chopped shallots, one table-spoon of chervil, and one-quarter pint of white wine and tarragon vinegar, mixed in equal quantities. Reduce the vinegar by two-thirds; add one pint of white wine sauce (111); boil for a few minutes; rub through a fine sieve, and finish the sauce with a sufficient quantity of herb juice (183) and one teaspoon of chopped chervil and tarragon. This sauce accompanies various fish.

108—VILLEROY SAUCE   *Sauce Villeroy*

Put into a saucepan one pint of Allemande Sauce (27) to which have been added two tablespoons of truffle *essence* and as much ham *essence*.

Reduce on an open fire and constantly stir until the sauce is sufficiently thick to coat immersed solids thickly.

109—VILLEROY SOUBISE SAUCE   *Sauce Villeroy Soubisée*

Put into a saucepan two-thirds pint of Allemande Sauce (27) and one-third pint of Soubise *purée* (105). Reduce as in the preceding case, as the uses to which this is put are the same. Now, according to the circumstances and the nature of the dish it is intended for, a few teaspoons of very black, chopped truffles may be added to this sauce.

110—VILLEROY TOMATOED SAUCE   *Sauce Villeroy Tomatée*

Prepare the sauce as explained under (108) and add to it the third of its volume of very fine tomato *purée* (29). Reduce in the same way.

Remarks.—Villeroy sauce, of any kind, is solely used for the coating of preparations said to be "à la Villeroy."

The Villeroy Tomato may be finally seasoned with curry or paprika. according to the preparation for which it is intended.

111—WHITE WINE SAUCE   *Sauce au Vin Blanc*

The three following methods are employed in making it:—

1. Add one-quarter pint of fish *fumet* to one pint of thickened

Velouté (27), and reduce by half. Finish the sauce, away from the fire, with four oz. of butter. Thus prepared, this white wine sauce is suitable for *glazed* fish.

2. Almost entirely reduce one-quarter pint of fish *fumet*. To this reduction add the yolks of four eggs, mixing them well, and follow with one lb. of butter, added by degrees, paying heed to the precautions indicated under sauce Hollandaise (30).

3. Put the yolks of five eggs into a small saucepan and mix them with one tablespoon of cold fish-stock. Put the pan in a water-bath and finish the sauce with one lb. of butter, meanwhile adding from time to time, and in small quantities, six tablespoons of excellent fish *fumet*. The procedure in this sauce is, in short, exactly that of the Hollandaise, with this distinction, that here fish *fumet* takes the place of the water.

Hot English and American Sauces .

112—APPLE SAUCE   *Sauce aux Pommes*

Quarter, peel, core, and chop two lbs. of medium-sized apples; place these in a saucepan with one tablespoon of powdered sugar, a bit of cinnamon, and a few tablespoons of water. Cook the whole gently with lid on, and smooth the *purée* with a whisk before serving.

Serve this sauce lukewarm with duck, goose, roast hare, etc.

113—BREAD SAUCE   *Sauce de Pain*

Boil one pint of milk, and add three oz. of fresh, white breadcrumbs, a little salt, a small onion with a clove stuck in it, and one oz. of butter. Cook gently for about a quarter of an hour, remove the onion, smooth the sauce by beating, and finish it with a few tablespoons of cream.

This sauce is served with roast fowl and roast feathered game.

114—CELERY SAUCE   *Sauce Céleri*

Clean six stalks of celery (only use the hearts), put them in a saucepan, immerse in consommé, add a herb bunch and one onion with a clove stuck in it, and cook gently. Drain the celery, put it through a grinder, then rub it through a fine sieve and put the *purée* in a saucepan. Now thin the *purée* with an equal quantity of cream sauce and a little reduced celery liquor. Heat it moderately, and, if it has to wait, put it in a double-boiler.

This sauce is suited to boiled or *braised* poultry. It is excellent, and has been adopted in French cookery.

115—CRANBERRY SAUCE   *Sauce aux Airelles*

Cook one pint of cranberries with one quart of water in a saucepan, and cover. When the berries are cooked mash them through a fine sieve. To the *purée* add the necessary quantity of their cooking liquor, so as to make a somewhat thick sauce. Sugar should be added according to taste.

This sauce is mostly served with roast turkey. It can be bought ready-made, and, if this kind be used, it need only be heated with a little water.

116—FENNEL SAUCE   *Sauce Fenouil*

Take one pint of butter sauce (66) and finish it with two table-spoons of chopped fennel, scalded for a few seconds.

This is principally used with mackerel.

117—EGG SAUCE WITH MELTED BUTTER
Sauce aux Oeufs au Beurre Fondu

Dissolve one-quarter pound of butter, and add to it the necessary salt, a little pepper, half the juice of a lemon, and three hard-boiled eggs (hot and cut into large cubes); also a teaspoon of chopped and scalded parsley.

118—SCOTCH EGG SAUCE   *Sauce Ecossaise*

Make a white *roux* (21) with one and one-half oz. of butter and one oz. of flour. Mix in one pint of boiling milk, season with salt, white pepper, and nutmeg, and boil gently for ten minutes. Then add three hot hard-boiled eggs, cut into cubes (the whites and the yolks).

This sauce usually accompanies boiled fish, especially fresh haddocks and fresh and salted cod.

119—HORSE-RADISH OR ALBERT SAUCE
Sauce Raifort ou Albert

Grate five oz. of horse-radish and place in a saucepan with one-quarter pint of white consommé (1). Boil gently for twenty minutes and add a good one-half pint of butter sauce (66), as much cream, and one-half oz. of bread-crumbs; thicken by reducing on a brisk fire and rub through a fine sieve. Then thicken with the yolks of two eggs, and complete the seasoning with a pinch of salt and pepper, and a teaspoon of dry mustard dissolved in a tablespoon of vinegar.

Serve this sauce with *braised* or roast beef—especially fillets.

119a—PARSLEY SAUCE   *Sauce Persil*

This is the Butter Sauce (66), to which is added, per pint, a heaped tablespoon of freshly-chopped parsley.

120—REFORM SAUCE   *Sauce Réforme*

Put into a small saucepan and boil one pint of half-glaze sauce (23) and one-half pint of ordinary Poivrade sauce (19). Complete with a garnish composed of one-half oz. of gherkins, one-half oz. of the hard-boiled white of an egg, one oz. of smoked tongue, one oz. of truffles, and one oz. of mushrooms. All these to be cut *julienne-*fashion and short.

This sauce is for mutton cutlets when these are "à la Reforme" (1316a).

CHAPTER IV

COLD SAUCES AND COMPOUND BUTTERS

121—AIOLI SAUCE OR PROVENCE BUTTER

Sauce Aïoli ou Beurre Provençale

Chop one oz. of garlic cloves as finely as possible, and add the yolk of one raw egg, a pinch of salt, and one-half pint of oil, letting it trickle in a thread and stirring meanwhile, so as to effect a complete cohesion of the mixture. Add a few drops of lemon juice and cold water to the sauce as it thickens, this being done to avoid its turning.

Should it separate in the process of making or when made, the only thing to be done is to begin again with another egg yolk.

122—ANDALOUSE SAUCE   *Sauce Andalouse*

Take the required quantity of Mayonnaise sauce (126) and add to it the quarter of its volume of very red and concentrated tomato *purée* (29), and finally add two oz. of pimento cut finely, *Julienne*-fashion, per pint of sauce.

123—BOHEMIAN SAUCE   *Sauce Bohémienne*

Put in a bowl one-quarter pint of cold Béchamel (28), the yolks of four eggs, a little table salt and white pepper. Add a quart of oil and three tablespoons of tarragon vinegar, proceeding as for the Mayonnaise (126).

Finish the sauce with a tablespoon of dry mustard.

124—GENOA SAUCE   *Sauce Génoise*

Pound in a mortar, and make into a smooth, fine paste, one oz of pistachios and one oz. of pine-nuts, or, if these are not available, one oz. of sweet almonds; add one-half tablespoon of cold Béchamel (28). Put this paste into a bowl, add the yolks of six eggs, a little salt and pepper, and finish the sauce with one quart of oil, the juice of two lemons, and proceed as for the Mayonnaise (126).

Complete with three tablespoons of *purée* of herbs (132), prepared with equal quantities of chervil, parsley, tarragon, and fresh pimpernel, scalded for one minute. Cool quickly, press so as to expel the water, and pass through a fine sieve.

Serve this sauce with cold fish.

125—GRIBICHE SAUCE   *Sauce Gribiche*

Crush in a bowl the yolks of six hard-boiled eggs, and work them into a smooth paste, together with a large tablespoon of French mustard, the necessary salt, a little pepper, and make up the sauce with one pint of oil. Complete with two teaspoons of parsley, chervil, and tarragon (chopped and mixed), as many capers and gherkins, evenly mixed, and the hard-boiled whites of three eggs, cut in short, *Julienne* strips.

This sauce is chiefly used with cold fish.

126—MAYONNAISE SAUCE   *Sauce Mayonnaise*

Put in a bowl the yolks of six raw eggs, after having removed the cores. Season them with one-half oz. of table-salt and a little cayenne pepper. Gradually pour one-fifth pint of vinegar on the yolks while beating them briskly. When the vinegar is absorbed add one quart of oil, letting the latter trickle down in a thread, constantly stirring the sauce meanwhile. The sauce is finished by the addition of the juice of a lemon and three tablespoons of boiling water—the purpose of the latter being to ensure the cohesion of the sauce and to prevent it separating.

Mayonnaise prepared in this way is rather liquid, but it need only be left to rest a few hours in order to thicken considerably. Unless it be exposed to too low a temperature, the Mayonnaise, prepared as above, never separates, and may be kept for several days without the fear of anything happening to it. Merely cover it and put away.

Remarks.—In the matter of that sauce there exist endless prejudices, which I must attempt to refute:—

1. If the sauce mixes badly, or not at all, the reason is that the oil has been added too rapidly at first, before the addition of the vinegar, and that its assimilation by the yolks has not functioned normally.

2. It is quite an error to suppose that it is necessary to work over ice or in a cold room. Cold is rather injurious to Mayonnaise, and is invariably the cause of this sauce separating in winter. In the cold season the oil should be slightly warmed, or, at least, kept at the

temperature of the kitchen, though it is best to make it in a moderately warm place.

3. It is a further error to suppose that the seasoning interferes with the making of the sauce, for salt, in solution, rather aids the cohering force of the yolks.

Causes of the Separation of the Mayonnaise:—

1. The too rapid addition of the oil at the start.

2. The use of congealed, or too cold, an oil.

3. Excess of oil in proportion to the number of yolks, the assimilating power of an egg being limited to two and one-half oz. of oil (if the sauce be made some time in advance), and three oz. if it is to be used immediately.

Means of Bringing Separated Mayonnaise Back to its Normal State.—Put the yolks of an egg into a bowl with a few drops of vinegar, and mix the separated Mayonnaise in it, little by little. If it be a matter of only a small quantity of Mayonnaise, one-half a teaspoon of prepared mustard can take the place of the egg-yolk. Finally, with regard to acid seasoning, a whiter sauce is obtained by the use of lemon juice instead of vinegar.

127—CLEARED MAYONNAISE SAUCE   *Sauce Mayonnaise Collée*

Take the necessary quantity of Mayonnaise (126) and gradually add to it, per one and one-half pints of the sauce, one-half pint of cold and rather firm melting aspic jelly—*Lenten* or ordinary, according to the nature of the products for which the sauce is intended.

Remarks.—It is this very Mayonnaise, formerly used almost exclusively for coating entrées and cold *relevées* of fish, filleted fish, scallops of common and spiny-lobster, etc., which I have replaced with the *Lenten* Chaud-Froid (76).

128—WHISKED MAYONNAISE   *Sauce Mayonnaise Broyée*

Put into a copper basin or other bowl three-quarters pint of melted jelly aspic, two-thirds pint of Mayonnaise (126), one tablespoon of tarragon vinegar, and as much grated or finely-chopped horse-radish. Mix up the whole and place the utensil on ice, and beat gently until the contents become very frothy. Stop beating as soon as the sauce begins to solidify, for it must remain almost liquid to enable it to mix with the foods for which it is intended.

This sauce is used principally for vegetable salads.

129—RAVIGOTE SAUCE, OR VINAIGRETTE

Sauce Ravigote, ou Vinaigrette

Put into a bowl one pint of oil, one-third pint of vinegar, a little salt and pepper, two oz. of small capers, three tablespoons of fine herbs, comprising some very finely chopped onion, as much parsley, and half as much chervil, tarragon, and chives. Mix thoroughly. The Ravigote accompanies calf's head or feet, sheep's shanks, etc.

Two or three tablespoons of the liquor or stock with which the accompanying foods have been cooked, are often added to this sauce when serving.

130—REMOULADE SAUCE   *Sauce Remoulade*

To one pint of Mayonnaise (126) add one large tablespoon of prepared mustard, another of gherkins, and yet another of chopped and pressed out capers, one tablespoon of fine herbs, parsley, chervil, and tarragon, all chopped and mixed, and a teaspoon of anchovy *essence* or a bit of anchovy paste.

This sauce accompanies cold meat and poultry, and more particularly, common and spiny lobster.

131—GREEN SAUCE   *Sauce Verte*

Take the necessary quantity of thick Mayonnaise (126) and spicy seasoning, and add to these, per pint of sauce, one-third pint of herb juice (132).

This is suitable for cold fish and shell fish.

132—VINCENT SAUCE   *Sauce Vincent*

Prepare and carefully wash the following herbs:—One oz. each of parsley, chervil, tarragon, chives, sorrel-leaves, and fresh pimpernel, two oz. of water-cress and two oz. of spinach. Put all these herbs into a copper bowl containing salted, boiling water. Boil for two minutes only; then drain the herbs through a sieve and cover them with fresh water. When they are cold they are once more drained until quite dry; then they must be finally chopped with the yolks of eight hard-boiled eggs. Rub this *purée* through a strainer first, then through a fine sieve, add one pint of very stiff Mayonnaise (126) to it and finish the sauce with two teaspoons of Worcestershire sauce.

COLD ENGLISH AND AMERICAN SAUCES

133—CAMBRIDGE SAUCE *Sauce Cambridge*

Pound together the yolks of six hard-boiled eggs, the washed and dried fillets of four anchovies, a teaspoon of capers, two teaspoons of chervil, tarragon, and chives, mixed. When the whole forms a fine paste, add one tablespoon of mustard, one-fifth pint of oil, one tablespoon of vinegar, and proceed as for a Mayonnaise (126). Season with a little cayenne; rub through a fine sieve, applying pressure with a spoon, and put the sauce in a bowl. Stir it awhile with a whisk to smooth it, and finish with one teaspoon of chopped parsley.

It is suited to cold meats in general; in fact, it is an Anglicized version of Vincent Sauce (132).

134—CUMBERLAND SAUCE *Sauce Cumberland*

Dissolve four tablespoons of red-currant jelly, to which are added one-fifth pint of port wine, one teaspoon of finely-chopped shallots, scalded for a few seconds and pressed, one teaspoon of small pieces of orange rind and as much lemon rind (cut finely, *Julienne*-fashion, scalded for two minutes, well-drained, and cooled), the juice of an orange and that of half a lemon, one teaspoon of dry mustard, a little cayenne pepper, and as much powdered ginger. Mix the whole well.

Serve this sauce with cold venison.

135—GLOUCESTER SAUCE *Sauce Gloucester*

Take one pint of very thick Mayonnaise (126) and complete it with one-fifth pint of sour cream with the juice of a lemon added, and combine with the Mayonnaise by degrees; one teaspoon of chopped fennel leaves and as much Worcestershire sauce.

Serve this with all cold meats.

136—MINT SAUCE *Sauce de Menthe*

Cut finely, *Julienne*-fashion, or chop, two oz. of mint leaves. Put these in a bowl with a little less than one oz. of white granulated or powdered sugar, one-quarter pint of fresh vinegar, and four tablespoons of water.

Special sauce for hot or cold lamb.

137—OXFORD SAUCE *Sauce Oxford*

Make a Cumberland (134) with this difference: that the *Julienne* of orange and lemon rinds should be replaced by grated or finely-chopped rinds, and that the quantities of same should be less, *i.e.,* two-thirds of a teaspoonful of each.

138—HORSE-RADISH SAUCE   *Sauce au Raifort*

Dilute one tablespoon of mustard with two tablespoons of vinegar in a basin, and add one lb. of finely grated horse-radish, two oz. of powdered sugar, a little salt, one pint of cream, and one lb. of bread-crumbs steeped in milk and pressed out. Stir this together vigorously. Serve this sauce very cold.

It accompanies boiled and roast joints of beef.

COMPOUND BUTTER FOR GRILLS AND FOR THE COMPLETION OF SAUCES

With the exception of those of the shell-fish order, the butters, whose recipes I am about to give, are not greatly used in kitchens. Nevertheless, in some cases, as, for instance, in accentuating the savor of sauces, they answer a real and useful purpose, and I therefore recommend them, since they enable one to give a flavor to the derivatives of the Velouté (25) and Béchamel (28) sauces which these could not acquire by any other means.

With regard to shell-fish butters, and particularly those of the common and spiny lobster (Rock lobsters) and the crayfish, experience has shown that when they are prepared with heat (that is to say, by melting in a double-boiler a quantity of butter which has been previously pounded with shell-fish remains and afterwards strained through muslin into a basin of ice water where it has solidified) they are of a finer color than the other kind and quite free from shell particles. But the heat, besides dissipating a large proportion of their delicacy, involves considerable risk, for the slightest neglect gives the above preparation quite a disagreeable taste. To obviate these difficulties I have adopted a system of two distinct butters, one which is colorful and prepared with heat, and the other which is prepared with all the creamy parts, the trimmings and the remains of common and spiny lobsters (Rock lobsters) without the shells, pounded with the required quantity of fresh butter and passed through a sieve. The latter is used to complete sauces, particularly those with a Béchamel base to which it lends a perfect savor.

I follow the same procedure with shrimp and crayfish butters, sometimes substituting for the butter good cream, which, I find, absorbs the aromatic principles perhaps better than the former.

With the above method it is advisable to pass the butter or the cream through a very fine strainer first and afterwards through a very fine sieve, so as to avoid small particles of the pounded shell being present in the sauce.

139—BERCY BUTTER   *Beurre Bercy*

Put into a small saucepan one-quarter pint of white wine and one oz. of finely-chopped shallots, scalded a moment. Reduce the wine· by one-half, and add one-half lb. of butter softened into a cream; one teaspoon of chopped parsley, two oz. of beef marrow cut into cubes, *poached* in slightly salted water and well drained, the necessary table-salt, and, when serving, add a little ground pepper and a few drops of lemon-juice.

This butter must not be completely melted, and it is principally served with grilled beef.

140—CHIVRY OR RAVIGOTE BUTTER   *Beurre Chivry ou Ravigote*

Put into a small saucepan of salted, boiling water six oz. of chervil, parsley, tarragon, fresh pimpernel, and chives, in equal quantities, and two oz. of chopped shallots. Boil quickly for two minutes, drain, cool in cold water, press in a towel to completely remove the water, and pound in a mortar. Now add one-half lb. of half-melted butter, mix well with the *purée* of herbs (132), and strain through a fine sieve.

This butter is used to complete Chivry sauce and other sauces that contain herb juices, such as the Venetian, etc.

140a—CHÂTEAUBRIAND BUTTER   *Beurre Châteaubriand*

Reduce by two-thirds four-fifths pint of white wine containing four chopped shallots, fragments of thyme and bay leaf, and four oz. of mushroom peelings. Add four-fifths pint of veal gravy, reduce the whole to half, rub it through a fine sieve, and finish it away from the fire with eight oz. of Maître d'Hôtel butter (150) and half a tablespoon of chopped tarragon.

141—COLBERT BUTTER   *Beurre Colbert*

Take one lb. of Maître d'Hôtel butter (150) and add six tablespoons of dissolved, pale meat *glaze* (15) and one teaspoon of chopped tarragon.

Serve this sauce with fish prepared à la Colbert.

142—RED COLORING BUTTER   *Beurre Rouge*

Put on to a dish any available left over shells of shell-fish after having thoroughly cleaned them of meat and dried them in the oven. Pound them until they form a very fine powder, and add their weight of butter.

Put the whole into a double-boiler and melt, stirring frequently. When the butter is quite clear strain it through muslin, twisting the latter over a tureen of ice water in which the strained butter solidifies. Put the congealed butter in a towel, press it heavily so as to expel the water, and keep cool in a small bowl.

Remarks.—A very fine and decided red color is obtained by using paprika as a condiment for sauces intended for poultry and certain meats, in accordance with the procedure I recommend for Hungarian paprika. But only the very best quality of paprika should be used—that which is mild and at the same time produces a nice pink color without entailing any excess of the condiment.

143—GREEN COLORING BUTTER   *Beurre Vert*

Peel, wash, and thoroughly shake (so as to get rid of every drop of water) two lbs. of spinach. Pound it raw and then press it in a strong towel, twisting the latter so as to extract all the vegetable juice. Pour this juice into a double-boiler and let it coagulate, and then pour it on to a napkin stretched over a bowl in order to drain away the water. Collect the remains of the coloring substance on the napkin, using a spatula for the purpose, and put these into a mortar; mix with half the weight of butter, strain through a fine sieve, and put aside to cool. This green butter should in all cases take the place of the liquid green found on the market.

144—VARIOUS CULLISES   *Coulis Divers*

Finely pound shrimp and crayfish shells, and combine with these the available creamy parts and spawn of the common and spiny or Rock lobsters; add one-quarter pint of rich cream per lb. of the above remains, and strain, first through a fine sieve and then through a fine hair sieve. This *cullis* is prepared just in time for serving, and is used as a refining element in certain fish sauces.

145—SHRIMP BUTTER   *Beurre de Crevette*

Finely pound any available shrimp remains, add to these their weight of butter, and strain through a fine sieve. Place in a bowl and put aside to chill.

146—SHALLOT BUTTER   *Beurre d'Echalote*

Put eight oz. of roughly minced shallots in the corner of a clean towel, and wash them quickly in boiling water. Cool, and press them heavily. Then pound them finely with their own weight of fresh butter and strain through a very fine sieve.

This butter accentuates the savor of certain sauces, such as Bercy, Ravigote, etc.

147—CRAYFISH BUTTER   *Beurre d'Ecrevisse*

Pound, very finely, the remains and shells of crayfish cooked in *Mirepoix*. Add their weight of butter, and strain through a fine sieve, and again through a fine hair sieve, so as to avoid the presence of any shell particles. This latter precaution applies to all shell-fish butters.

148—TARRAGON BUTTER   *Beurre d'Estragon*

Quickly scald and cool eight oz. of fresh tarragon, drain, press in a towel, pound in a mortar, and add to them one lb. of butter. Strain through a very fine sieve, and put aside to chill if it is not to be used immediately.

149—LOBSTER BUTTER   *Beurre de Homard*

Reduce to a paste in the mortar the spawn, shell, and creamy parts of lobster. Add their equal in weight of butter and strain through a very fine sieve.

150—BUTTER A LA MAITRE D'HOTEL   *Beurre à la Maitre d'Hotel*

First *manie* and then soften into a cream one-half lb. of butter. Add a tablespoon of chopped parsley, a little salt and pepper, and a few drops of lemon-juice.

Serve this with grills in general.

151—MANIE BUTTER   *Beurre Manié*

Knead, until perfectly combined, four oz. of butter and three oz. of sifted flour. This butter is used for quick bindings like in the *Matelotes*, etc.

The sauce to which *manie* butter has been added should not boil too long if this can possibly be avoided, but long enough to cook the flour otherwise it would have a very disagreeable taste of uncooked flour.

151a—MELTED BUTTER *Beurre Fondu*

This preparation, which is used principally as a fish sauce, should consist of butter, just melted, and combined with a little table-salt and a few drops of lemon-juice. It should therefore be prepared only at the last minute; for, should it wait and be allowed to clarify, besides losing its flavor it will be found to disagree with certain people.

152—BUTTER A LA MEUNIERE *Beurre à la Meunière*

Put into a saucepan the necessary quantity of butter, and cook it gently until it has acquired a golden tint and exudes a slightly nutty odor. Add a few drops of lemon-juice, and pour on the fish being prepared, which should have been previously sprinkled with chopped parsley.

This butter is proper to fish "à la Meunière" and is always served on the fish.

153—MONTPELIER BUTTER *Beurre Montpelier*

Put into a saucepan containing boiling water equal quantities of watercress leaves, parsley, chervil, chives, and tarragon (six oz. in all), one and one-half oz. of chopped shallots, and one-half oz. of fresh spinach leaves. Boil for two minutes, then drain, cool, press in a towel to expel water, and pound in a mortar with one tablespoon of pressed capers, four oz. of gherkins, a garlic clove, and the fillets of four anchovies well washed.

Mix this paste with one and one-half lbs. of butter; then add the yolks of three boiled eggs and two raw eggs, and finally pour in, by degrees, two-fifths pint of oil. Strain through a very fine sieve, put the butter into a bowl, and stir it well with a wooden spoon to make it smooth. Season with table-salt and a little cayenne.

Use this butter to decorate large fish, such as salmon and trout; but it is also used for smaller pieces and slices of fish.

Remarks.—When this butter is specially prepared to form a coating on fish, the oil and the egg yolks are omitted and only butter is used.

154—BLACK BUTTER *Beurre Noir*

Put into a saucepan the necessary amount of butter, and cook it until it has assumed a brown color and begins to smoke. At this moment add a large pinch of chopped parsley leaves and spread it immediately over the object to be treated.

155—HAZEL-NUT BUTTER   *Beurre de Noisette*

Put eight oz. of shelled hazel-nuts, in the front of the oven, in order to slightly grill their skins and make them easily removable. Now crush the nuts in a mortar until they form a paste, and add a few drops of cold water with a view to preventing their producing any oil. Add an equal weight of butter and rub through a fine sieve.

156—PISTACHIO BUTTER   *Beurre de Pistache*

Put into boiling water eight oz. of pistachio nuts, and heat them over the fire until the peel may be easily removed. Drain, cool in cold water, clean the pistachios, and finely pound while moistening them with a few drops of water.

Add two oz. of butter and pass through a fine sieve.

157—PRINTANIER BUTTER   *Beurre Printanier*

These butters are made from all early-season vegetables, such as carrots, string beans, peas, and asparagus tips.

When dealing with green vegetables cook quickly in boiling, salted water, drain, dry, pound with their weight of butter, and rub through a fine sieve.

With carrots: Mince and cook with consommé, a little sugar, and butter until the liquid is quite reduced. After cooling they are pounded with their own weight of butter and rubbed through a fine sieve.

CHAPTER V

Aspic jellies are to cold cookery what consommés and stock are to hot. If anything, the former are perhaps more important, for a cold entrée—however perfect it may be in itself—is nothing without its accompanying jelly or aspic.

In the recipes which I give hereafter I have made a point of showing how melting jellies may be obtained, that is, served in a sauceboat simultaneously with the cold food, or actually poured over it when the latter rests in a deep dish—a common custom nowadays.

This method of serving cold entrées, which I inaugurated at the Savoy Hotel in London with the "Suprême de Volaille Jeannette," is the only one which permits serving an aspic jelly in a state of absolute perfection.

Nevertheless, if a more solid jelly were required, either for the decorating of cold dishes or for a moulded entrée, there need only be added to the following recipes a few tablespoons of granulated gelatine—more or less—according to the required firmness of the aspic.

But it should not be forgotten that the greater the glutinous consistency of the jelly the less value will the same possess.

The various uses of aspics are dealt with in Part II. of this work, where the recipes of their various accompanying dishes will also appear.

158—ORDINARY ASPICS   *Gelées Ordinaires*

Stock for Ordinary Aspic—Quantities for Making Four Quarts

4 lbs. of tied knuckle of veal.	3 calf's feet, boned and *blanched.*
3 lbs. of tied knuckle of beef.	
3 lbs. of veal bones, well broken up.	$\frac{1}{2}$ lb. of fresh pork rind, well *blanched* and with fat removed.

Mode of Procedure.—Put the meat in a very clean stockpot or saucepan. Add eight quarts of cold water, boil, and skim after the manner indicated under (1). Having well skimmed the stock add one oz. of salt, put it on a low fire, and let it boil gently for four hours. Then remove the meat, taking care not to disturb the stock. Carefully remove the fat, and garnish with one-half lb. of carrots, six oz. of onions, two oz. of leeks, a stalk of celery, and a large herb bunch. Put the whole back on to the fire and cook gently for a further two hours. Strain through a sieve into a very clean bowl and leave it to cool.

Clarification of Aspic.—When the stock, prepared according to the above directions, has cooled, the grease that has formed on its surface should be removed. Then pour off gently into a saucepan of convenient size in such a way as to prevent the deposit at the bottom from mixing with the clear liquor. Test the consistency of the aspic, when it should be found that the quantities given above have proved sufficient to form a fairly firm jelly. If, however, this be not the case, a few ounces of granulated gelatine steeped in cold water should be added, being careful not to overdo the quantity. Now add to the stock two lbs. of lean beef (first minced and then ground together with the white of an egg), a little chervil and tarragon, and a few drops of lemon-juice. Place the saucepan on a fire, stir its contents with a spatula until the liquid begins to boil, remove it from the fire, and place it on a low flame, where it may boil gently for half an hour longer.

At the end of this time take the saucepan off the fire and remove what little grease has formed on the aspic while cooking. Strain through a napkin stretched across a frame and let the aspic fall into a bowl placed beneath it. Make certain whether the liquid is quite clear, and if, as frequently happens, this be not the case, what has already been strained should once more be passed through the napkin, repeating the operation until the aspic becomes quite transparent.

Flavoring the Aspic.—The aspic obtained as above is transparent, has an agreeable savor, and is the color of fine amber. It now only requires flavoring according to the tastes of the consumer and the purpose for which it is intended. For this operation it should be allowed to become quite tepid, and the following quantities of choice wine are added to it, viz.:—

If the wine is of a liqueur kind, such as Sherry, Marsala, Madeira, etc., one-fifth pint per quart.

If it is another kind of wine, for example, champagne, hock, etc., one-fourth pint per quart.

The wine used should be very clear, free from any deposit and as perfect as possible in taste.

159—CHICKEN ASPIC *Gelée de Volaille*

The quantities of meat are the same as for ordinary aspic; there need only be added to it either two oven-browned hens, or their equivalent in weight of roasted fowl skeletons, and poultry giblets if these are handy. It is always better, however, to prepare the stock with the hens and giblets and to keep the skeletons for the clarification. This clarification follows the same rules as that of the ordinary aspic, except that a few roasted-fowl skeletons, previously well freed from fat, are added to it.

In the case of this particularly delicate aspic, it is more than ever necessary not to overdo the amount of gelatine. It should be easily soluble to the palate in order to be perfect.

160—GAME ASPIC *Gelée de Gibier*

Prepare this aspic stock in exactly the same way as that of ordinary aspic, only substitute game, such as deer, roebuck, doe, or hare, or wild rabbit (previously browned in the oven), for the beef. When possible also add to this stock a few old game birds, such as partridges or pheasants that are too tough for other purposes and which suit admirably here.

The clarification changes according to the different flavors which are to be given to the aspic. If it is not necessary to give it a special characteristic, it should be prepared with the meat of the game which happens to be most available at the time, adding to the quantity used roast bones and pickings of game birds, the respective amounts of both ingredients being the same as for ordinary aspic. If, on the other hand, the aspic is to have a well-defined flavor, the meat used for the clarification should naturally be that producing the flavor in question, either partridge or pheasant, or grouse, etc.

Some aspics are greatly improved by being flavored with a small quantity of old brandy. Rather than use an inferior kind of this ingredient, however, I should advise its total omission from the aspic.

Without flavoring the aspic, though imperfect, is passable; but flavored with bad brandy it is invariably spoilt.

LENTEN ASPICS

161—FISH ASPIC WITH WHITE WINE *Gelée de Poisson au Vin Blanc*

The stock for this aspic is prepared in precisely the same manner as fish stock (4). The saucepan need not, however, be buttered previous to the adding of the onions, parsley-stalks, and fish-bones. If the aspic is not required to be quite white, a little saffron may be added to it, as the flavor of this condiment blends so perfectly with that of fish.

When the stock is prepared its consistency should be tested, and rectified, if necessary, by means of gelatine. The quantity of this substance should on no account exceed three and three-quarters ounces per quart of aspic, and, at the risk of repeating myself, I remind the reader that the less gelatine is used the better the aspic will be.

The clarification should be made with fresh caviar if possible, but pressed caviar is also admirably suited to this purpose. The quantities are the same as for the clarification of fish consommé (4).

In flavoring white fish aspics either dry champagne or a good Bordeaux or Burgundy may be used. Take care, however—

1. That the wine used be of an unquestionably good quality.

2. That it be only added to the aspic when the latter is already cold and on the point of coagulating, as this is the only means of preserving all the aroma of the wine.

Finally, in certain cases, a special flavor may be obtained by the use of crayfish, which are cooked, as for *bisque,* then pounded, and added to the fish stock (11) ten minutes before straining it. A proportion of four little crayfish *à bisque* per quart of aspic is sufficient to secure an excellent flavor.

162—FISH ASPIC WITH RED WINE *Gelée de Poisson au Vin Rouge*

This aspic stock is the *Court-bouillon* with red wine (165), which has served in cooking the fish for which the aspic is intended; this fish is generally either trout or salmon; sometimes also, but less commonly, a carp or a pike.

This stock must first of all have its grease thoroughly removed; it should then be carefully poured off, reduced if necessary, and the required quantity of gelatine added. This cannot be easily determined, as all gelatines are not alike, and the stock may have contracted a certain consistency from its contact with the fish. One can, therefore, only be guided by testing small quantities cooled in ice, but care should be taken that the aspic be not too firm.

The clarification of this aspic is generally made with white of egg in the proportion of one white per quart. The white, slightly beaten, is added to the cold stock, and the latter is put over a fire and stirred with a spatula. As soon as it boils, the aspic is poured through a napkin on a frame. The first drippings of the fluid aspic are put back through the napkin if they do not seem clear, and this operation is repeated until the required clarity is reached.

It almost invariably happens that, either during the cooking of the fish or during the clarification, the wine loses its color through the precipitation of the coloring elements derived from the tannin.

The only way of overcoming this difficulty is to add a few drops of liquid carmine or red vegetable coloring; but, in any case, it is well to remember that the color of red-wine aspic must never be deeper than a dark pink.

CHAPTER VI

163—COURT-BOUILLON WITH VINEGAR   *Court-Bouillon au Vinaigre*

COURT-BOUILLON AU VIN BLANC

Quantities Required for Five Quarts

5 quarts of water.
½ pint of vinegar.
2 oz. of salt.
½ oz. of peppercorns.

¾ lb. of carrots.
1 lb. of onions.
A little thyme and bay leaf.
2 oz. of parsley stalks.

Preparation.—Put into a saucepan the water, salt, and vinegar, the minced carrots and onions, and the parsley, thyme, and bay leaf, in a bunch. Bring to a boil, allow to simmer for one hour, rub through a fine sieve, and put aside until wanted.

Remarks.—Put the peppercorns into the court-bouillon only twelve minutes before straining the latter. If the pepper were in for too long a time it would give a bitterness to the preparation. This rule also applies to the recipes that follow, in which the use of pepper-corns is also required.

This court-bouillon is principally used for cooking trout and salmon, as well as for various shell-fish.

164—COURT-BOUILLON WITH WHITE WINE

Court-Bouillon au Vin Blanc

Quantities Required for Two Quarts

1 quart of white wine.
1 quart of water.
3 oz. of minced onions.

1 large herb bunch.
½ oz. of salt.
A few peppercorns.

Preparation.—This is the same as for the court-bouillon with vinegar, except that it is boiled for half an hour and is strained through a fine sieve.

Remarks.—If the court-bouillon has to be reduced the quantity of salt should be proportionately less. This preparation is principally used for *poaching* fresh-water fish.

165—COURT-BOUILLON WITH RED WINE

Court-Bouillon au Vin Rouge

Use the same quantities as for court-bouillon with white wine, taking care—

1. To replace white wine by excellent red wine.
2. To add four oz. of minced carrots.
3. To apportion the wine and water in the ratio of two-thirds to one-third.

Preparation.—The same as that of the former, with the same time for boiling.

Remarks.—If the court-bouillon is to be reduced, the salt should be less accordingly. When the court-bouillon with red wine is to constitute an aspic stock, fish *fumet* with enough gelatine takes the place of the water.

The uses of court-bouillon with red wine are similar to those of the white-wine kind.

166—PLAIN COURT-BOUILLON　　*Court-Bouillon Ordinaire*

The quantity of court-bouillon is determined by the size of the food which it is to cover. It is composed of cold, salt water (the salt amounting to a little less than one-half oz. per quart of water), one-quarter pint of milk per quart of water, and one thin slice of peeled lemon in the same proportion. The fish is immersed while the liquor is cold; the latter is very slowly brought to the boil, and as soon as this is reached, the pot is moved to the slowest fire, where the cooking of the fish is completed.

This court-bouillon, which is used with large pieces of turbot, is never prepared beforehand.

167—SPECIAL OR WHITE COURT-BOUILLON

Court-Bouillon Special, ou Blanc

This preparation is a genuine court-bouillon, though it is not used in cooking fish.

*The Quantities Required for Five Quarts of this
Court-bouillon are:—*

A little less than 2 oz. of flour.   The juice of 3 lemons or ⅛ pint
1½ oz. of salt.   of good vinegar.
                                      5 quarts of cold water.

Gradually mix the flour and the water; add the salt and the lemon
juice, and pass through a strainer. Set to boil, and stir the mixture,
in order to prevent the flour from lumping; as soon as the boil is
reached, immerse the objects to be treated. These are usually calf's
head or feet, previously *blanched*; sheep's shanks, cock's kidneys or
combs, or such vegetables as salsify, oyster plant, cardoon, etc.

Remarks upon the Use of Court-bouillon

1. Court-bouillon must always be prepared in advance for all fish,
as the time for *poaching* is less than half an hour, except turbots.

2. When a fish is of such a size as to need more than half an hour's
poaching, proceed as follows:—Place under the trivet or drainer of
the fish-kettle the minced carrots and onions and the herb bunch;
put the fish on the trivet, and cover it with water and vinegar, or
white wine, in accordance with the kind of court-bouillon wanted
and the quantity required. Add the salt, boil, and keep the court-
bouillon gently simmering for a period of time according to the size
of the fish. The time allowed for *poaching* will be given in the
respective recipes.

3. Fish, when whole, should be immersed in cold court-bouillon;
when sliced, in the same liquor that is boiling. The exceptions to
this rule are small trout *"au bleu"* and shell-fish.

4. If fish be cooked in a small amount of liquor the carrots,
onions, etc. are put under the drainer and the liquid elements of the
selected court-bouillon (as, for example, that with red or white wine)
are so calculated as to cover only one-third of the solid body. Fish
cooked in this way should be frequently basted.

5. Court-bouillon for ordinary and spiny (Rock) lobsters should
always be at full boiling pitch when these are immersed. The case is
the same for small or medium fish *"au bleu."*

6. Fish which is to be served cold, also shell-fish (crustaceans),
should cool in the court-bouillon itself; the cooking period is consequently curtailed.

MARINADES AND BRINES

Marinades play but a small part in English and American cookery, venison or other game being generally preferred fresh. However, in the event of its being necessary to resort to these methods of preparation, I shall give two recipes for venison and two for mutton.

The use of the *marinade* for venison is very much debated. Certainly it is often desirable that the fibre of those meats that come from old specimens of the deer be softened, but there is no doubt that what the meat gains in tenderness it loses in flavor. On the whole, therefore, it would be best to use only those joints which come from young beasts.

In the case of the latter, the *marinade* may well be dispensed with. It would add nothing to the savor of a haunch of venison, while it would be equally ineffectual in the case of the roebuck or hare. A summary treatment of these two, with raw *marinade*, may well be adopted, as also for deer.

As for cooked *marinade*, its real and only use lies in the fact that during summer weather it enables one to preserve meat which would otherwise spoil. It may, moreover, be used for *braised* venison, but this treatment of game is very uncommon nowadays.

168—COOKED MARINADE FOR VENISON
Marinade Cuite pour Venaison

Quantities Required for Five Quarts

½ lb. of minced carrots.
½ lb. of minced onions.
2 oz. of minced shallots.
1 crushed garlic clove.

1 herb bunch, including 1 oz. of parsley stalks, 2 sprigs of rosemary, as much thyme, and 2 bay leaves.

Preparation.—Heat one-half pint of oil in a saucepan, add the carrots and onions, and fry them while stirring frequently. When they begin to brown add the shallots, the garlic, and the herb bunch, then one pint of vinegar, two bottles of white wine, and three quarts of water. Cook this *marinade* for twenty minutes, and add a further two oz. of salt, one-half oz. of peppercorns, and four oz. of brown sugar. Ten minutes afterwards pass it through a strainer and let it cool before laying in the meats.

N.B.—In summer the *marinade* very often decomposes, because of the blood contained by the meat under treatment in it. The only means of averting this is to boil the *marinade* every two or three days at least and keeping it well chilled.

169—RAW MARINADE FOR MEAT OR VENISON

Marinade Crue pour Viandes ou Venaison

This *marinade* is prepared immediately before using. The meat to be treated is first salted and peppered on all sides, then it is put in a receptacle just large enough to hold it, and laid on a bed of *aromatics*, including minced carrots and onions, a few chopped shallots, parsley stalks, thyme, and bay leaf in proportion to the rest. Now sprinkle the meat copiously with oil and half as much vinegar; cover the dish with oiled paper, and put it somewhere to keep cool. Turn the meat over three or four times a day, covering it each time with a layer of vegetables.

This *marinade* is very active, and is admirably suited to all meat and venison, provided they are not allowed to remain in it for too long a time. It is very difficult to say how long the meat must stay in these *marinades*; the time varies according to the size and quality of the joints, and the taste of the consumer. All that can be said is that three hours should be sufficient to *marinate* a cutlet or pieces of roebuck, and that for big joints such as saddle or leg the time should not exceed four days.

170—MARINADE FOR MUTTON, ROEBUCK-STYLE

Marinade pour le Mouton, en Chevreuil

This is exactly the same as cooked *marinade* (168). There need only be added one oz. of juniper berries, a few sprigs of rosemary, wild thyme, and basil, two more garlic cloves, and one quart less of water.

171—MARINADE WITH RED WINE FOR MUTTON

Marinade pour le Mouton au Vin Rouge

By substituting red wine for white in the preceding recipe—the quantity of the liquid equalling that of the water—and by slightly increasing the quantity of *aromatics*, etc. an excellent *marinade* for mutton is obtained, which in summer enables one to preserve meat, otherwise perishable, for some days.

172—BRINE   *Grande Saumure*

Quantities Required for Fifty Quarts

56 lbs. of kitchen or rock salt   6 lbs. of saltpeter.
50 quarts of water.   3½ lbs. of brown sugar.

Mode of Procedure.—Put the salt and the water in a lined copper pan, and put it over an open fire. When the water boils, throw in a peeled potato, and, if it floats, add water until it begins to sink. If, on the contrary, the potato should sink immediately, reduce the liquid until it is able to buoy the potato up. At this stage the sugar and saltpeter are added; let them dissolve, and the brine is then removed from the fire and is allowed to cool. It is then poured into the receptacle intended for it, which must be either of earthenware, stone, or cement. It is well to place in the bottom of this reservoir a wooden lattice, where the meats to be salted may be laid, for, were the immersed objects to lie directly on the bottom of the receptacle, the under parts would be entirely shielded from the brine.

If the meats to be salted are of an appreciable size, they should be inoculated with brine by means of a special syringe. Without this measure it would be impossible to salt evenly, as the sides would already be over-saturated before the center had even been properly reached.

Eight days should be allowed for salting a piece of beef of any size, above eight or ten lbs., since the process of inoculation equalizes the salting.

Ox-tongue intended for salting, besides having to be as fresh as possible, must be trimmed of almost all the cartilage of the throat, and carefully pounded either with a wooden mallet or rolling pin. Then it must be pricked on all sides with a heavy needle, and immersed in the liquid, where it should be slightly weighted by some means or other in order to prevent its rising to the surface. A medium-sized tongue would need about seven days' immersion in the brine.

Though brine does not turn as easily as the cooked *marinades*, it would be well, especially in warm weather, to watch it and occasionally to boil it. But, as the process of boiling invariably concentrates the brine, a little water should be added to it every time it is so treated, and the test of the potato, described above, should always be resorted to. (Of course there is no reason to have spoilage today because of modern refrigeration.—Ed.)

CHAPTER VII

1. ELEMENTARY PREPARATIONS

BEFORE broaching the question of the numerous preparations which constitute the various soup, *relevés*, and entrée garnishes, it will be necessary to give the recipes of the elementary preparations, or what are technically called the *mise en place*. If the various operations which go to make the *mise en place* were not, at least summarily, discussed here, I should be compelled to repeat them in each formula for which they are required—that is to say, in almost every recipe. I should thus resemble those bad cooks who, having neglected their *mise en place*, are obliged to make it in the course of other work, and thereby not only run the risk of making it badly, but also of losing valuable time which might be used to better advantage.

Elementary preparations consist of those things of which one is constantly in need, which may be prepared in advance, and which are kept available for use at a moment's notice.

173—FILLETS OF ANCHOVIES *Filets d'Anchois*

Whether they be for hors d'œuvres or for culinary use, it is always best to have these handy.

After having washed and well wiped them, in order to remove the white powder resulting from the little scales with which they are covered, they should be neatly trimmed to the shape of extended oblongs. Then detach the fillets from the bones by gentle pulling, divide each fillet lengthwise into three or four smaller fillets, put the latter into a small narrow dish or a little bowl, and cover them with oil. The fillets may also be kept whole with a view to rolling them into rings.

174—ANGLAISE (FOR EGG-AND-BREAD-CRUMBLING)

Panés à l'Anglaise

It is well to have this always ready for those dishes which are to be *panés à l'anglaise* (breaded), or as many of the recipes direct: *treated à l'anglaise*.

It is made of well-beaten eggs, salt, pepper and one teaspoon of oil per egg.

Its Uses.—The solids to be *panés à l'anglaise* (breaded) are dipped into the preparation described above taking care that the latter coats them thoroughly; whereupon, according to the requirements, they are rolled either in bread-crumbs or in fine *raspings*. From this combination of egg with bread-crumbs or *raspings* there results a kind of coat which, at the moment of contact with the hot fat, is immediately converted into a resisting crust. In croquettes this crust checks the escape, into the fat, of the substances it encloses, and this is more especially the case when the croquettes contain some reduced sauce, or are composed of uncooked meats or fish whose juices are thereby entirely retained. A solid food prepared *à l'anglaise* and cooked in fat should always be put into the fat when this is very hot, so as to ensure the instantaneous solidification of the egg and bread-crumbs.

N.B.—Foods to be treated *à l'anglaise* are generally rolled in flour before being immersed in the *anglaise,* for the flour helps the bread-crumbs and egg to adhere to the food.

The crust formed over the food thus acquires a density which is indispensable.

174a—AROMATICS   *Aromatiques*

Aromatics play a very prominent part in cookery, and their combination with the condiments constitutes, as Grinod de la Reynière said, "the hidden soul of cooking." Their real object, in fact, is to throw the savor of dishes into relief, to intensify that savor, and to give each culinary preparation its particular stamp.

They are all derived from the vegetable kingdom; but, while some are used dry, others are used fresh.

The first-named should belong to the permanent kitchen stock; they are: *sage, basil, rosemary, sweet marjoram, thyme,* and *bay leaf.*

Also to be included in the permanent stock are: *cinnamon, ginger, juniper-berries, nutmeg, cloves, mace* and *vanilla bean.*

The last-named comprise those *aromatic* herbs used fresh, such as: *parsley, chervil, tarragon, pimpernel,* and *common savory;* while, under this head, there may also be included: bits of orange and lemon rind and *zests* of lemon.

174b—SEASONING AND CONDIMENTS   *Assaisonnement*

Seasonings are divided into several classes, which comprise:—

1. *Saline seasonings.*—Salt, spiced salt, saltpeter.

2. *Acid seasonings.*—Plain vinegar, or the same aromatized with tarragon; *verjuice,* lemon and orange juices.

3. *Hot seasonings.*—Peppercorns, ground or coarsely chopped pepper, or *mignonette* pepper; paprika, curry, cayenne, and mixed pepper spices.

4. *Saccharine seasonings.*—Sugar and honey.

Condiments are likewise subdivided, the three classes being:—

1. *The pungents.*—Onions, shallots, garlic, chives, and horse-radish.

2. *Hot condiments.*—Mustard, gherkins, capers, English sauces, such as Worcestershire, Harvey, Ketchup, Escoffier's sauces, etc. and American sauces such as Chili, Tabasco, A-One, Beefsteak, etc.; the wines used in reductions and *braisings;* the finishing elements of sauces and soups.

3. *Fatty substances.*—Most animal fats, butter, vegetable greases (edible oils and margarine).

Remarks.—In cookery it should be borne in mind that both excellence and edibility depend entirely upon a judicious use and a rational blending of the *aromatics,* seasonings, and condiments. And, according as the latter have been used and apportioned, their action will be either beneficial or injurious to the health of the consumer.

In the matter of seasoning there can be no question of approximation or half measures; the quantities must be exact, allowing only of slight elasticity in respect of the various tastes to be satisfied.

175—CLARIFIED BUTTER *Beurre Clarifié*

A certain quantity of clarified butter should always be kept ready and handy.

To prepare this butter, put one lb. to melt in a saucepan large enough to hold twice that amount. Place the saucepan on the fire, over moderate heat; remove all the scum which rises to the surface, and, when the butter looks quite clear and all foreign substances have dropped to the bottom, strain it through muslin and put the liquid carefully away.

176—HERB BUNCHES *Bouquets Garnis*

These little bunches of *aromatics* which, when the contrary is not stated, are generally composed (in order to weigh one ounce) of eight-tenths oz. of parsley sprigs and roots, one-tenth oz. of bay leaves, and one-tenth oz. of thyme. These various *aromatics* are tied neatly together so that no sprig of the one sticks out beyond the others.

177—CHERVIL   *Cerfeuil*

Chopped Chervil.—Clean the chervil and remove the stalks; wash, dry it well while tossing it, then chop it finely and put it aside on a plate in a cool place, if it is not for immediate use.

Concassed Chervil.—Proceed as above, except that, instead of chopping it, compress it between the fingers and slice it with a shredding knife. *Concassed* and chopped chervil are, if possible, only prepared at the last moment.

Chervil Pluches.—The pluches are greatly used in the finishing off of soups. They are, practically, the serrated portions only of the leaves, which are torn away in such a manner as to show no trace of the veinings. They are immersed in water, and at the last moment withdrawn, so as to be added, raw, to either soups or boiling consommés.

178—RASPINGS   *Chapelure*

Golden raspings are obtained by pounding and passing through a fine sieve bread-crusts which have been previously well dried in the oven.

White raspings are similarly prepared, except that very dry, white crumb is used.

179—PEELED, CHANNELLED, AND ZESTED LEMONS
Citrons, écorcés, creusés et zestés

Lemons are greatly used in cookery, as a decorative and edible garnish. When a whole lemon is used for marinades of fish, for the *"blancs,"* etc., it is well to remove the peel and the whole of the underlying white. The lemon is then cut into more or less large slices, according to the use for which it is intended.

The rind of a lemon thus peeled may be cut into bits and used in this form as the necessity arises. When cutting it up, flatten the rind inside uppermost on the table, and, with a very sharp and flexible knife, scrape off all the white; then slice the remaining peel (which constitutes what is called *zest*) into strips about one inch wide, and cut these across *julienne*-fashion.

Scald the bits of lemon for five minutes, cool them, drain them carefully, and put them aside until wanted. Sometimes, instead of cutting *julienne*-fashion, the *zest* may be finely chopped, but the rest of the process remains the same.

Lemons are grooved by means of a little knife, or a special instrument for the purpose, which cuts out parallel ribbons from the surface of the rind and lays the white bare. A lemon grooved in this way is cut in two, lengthwise with the core; its two ends are removed, and the two halves are cut across into thin, regular slices to look like serrated half-discs.

Fried fish, oysters, and certain game are generally garnished with lemon slices fashioned according to the taste of the cook; but the simplest, and perhaps the best, way is to cut the lemon through the center, after having trimmed the two ends quite straight, and then to remove the rind roughly from the edge.

For whatever purpose the lemon be intended, it should be, as far as possible, only prepared at the last moment. If it must be prepared beforehand, it would be well to keep it in a bowl of fresh water or covered in the refrigerator.

180—SHALLOTS *Echalotes*

Chopped Shallots.—Peel the shallots, and, by means of a very sharp knife, cut them lengthwise into thin slices; let these cling together by not allowing the knife to cut quite through them, and, this done, turn them half round and proceed in the same way at right angles to the other cuts.

Finally, cut them across, and this will be found to produce very fine and regular, small cubes.

Sliced Shallots.—These are merely sliced across, the result of which operation is a series of thin, regular slices. Chopped shallots should, when possible, only be prepared when required; if, however, they must be treated in advance, they should be kept somewhere in a cool place until wanted.

181—SPICES *Epices*

Strictly speaking, spices include cinnamon, nutmeg, ginger, mace; and the many varieties of peppers and pimentos, cayenne, paprika, etc.

These various condiments are found ready-made on the market, and they need only be kept dry in air-tight boxes in order to prevent the escape of their aroma.

But there is another kind of preparation, in cookery, to which the name of spice or all-spice is more especially given. Nowadays several market varieties of this preparation exist, and vie with each other for custom, though in most cases they deserve it equally well.

Formerly this was not so, and every chef had his own formula.

The following is a recipe for the spice in question, which would be found useful if it had to be prepared at a moment's notice:—

Obtain the following, very dry

5 oz. of bay leaves.	4 oz. of cloves.
3 oz. of thyme (half of it wild, if possible).	3 oz. of ginger-root.
	3 oz. of mace.
3 oz. of coriander.	10 oz. of mixed pepper (half
4 oz. of cinnamon.	black and half white).
6 oz. of nutmeg.	1 oz. of cayenne.

Put all these ingredients into a mortar and pound them until they are all able to pass through a very fine sieve. Put the resulting powder into an air-tight box, which must be kept dry.

Before being used, this spice is generally mixed with salt (188).

182—FLOUR   *Farine*

For whatever use the flour is intended, it is always best to sift it. This is more particularly necessary in the case of flour used for coating objects to be fried; for the latter, being first dipped into milk, must of necessity let a few drops of the milk fall into the flour they are rolled in. Lumps would therefore form, which might adhere to the objects to be fried if the flour were not sifted.

183—HERB JUICE   *Jus d'Herbes*

This is to finish or intensify certain preparations.

To prepare it, throw into a small saucepan of boiling water some parsley, chervil, and tarragon and chive leaves, in equal quantities, according to the amount of juice required.

Set to boil for two minutes, drain, cool, press the herbs in a towel, twisting it; pound very finely, and extract the juice from the resulting paste by twisting it in a strong towel.

Keep this juice in a cool place.

(In the United States the use of a juicer simplifies the method of obtaining herb juice.—Ed.)

184—BREAD-CRUMBS   *Mie de Pain*

Thoroughly rub, in a folded towel, some stale bread-crumbs well broken up. Pass them through a fine sieve or colander, according to whether they are required very fine or not, and put them aside in a convenient container.

185—CHOPPED ONION   *Oignon Haché*

Cut the onion finely, like the shallots, but if it is to be minced to make it even finer, it should be freed of its pungent juice, which would cause it to blacken with exposure to the air.

To accomplish this, put the onion in the corner of a towel, pour plenty of cold water over it, and twist the towel in order to press out the water. By this means the onion remains quite white.

186—TURNED OR PITTED OLIVES   *Olives Tournées en Spirale*

There are special instruments for pitting olives, but, lacking these, cut the fruit spirally from the pit with the point of a small knife.

Keep the olives in slightly salted water.

187—PARSLEY   *Persil*

Chopped Parsley.—If parsley be properly chopped, no juice should be produced. If, on the contrary, this is badly done, and amounts to a process of pounding which would press out the juice.

In the latter case the particles stick together, and they are sprinkled with difficulty over an object. To remedy this shortcoming, wash the choppings in fresh water, as in the case of the onion, pressing in a similar manner so as to expel the water.

Concassed Parsley is that kind which is roughly chopped. When a culinary preparation is dressed with *concassed* parsley, the latter should be added to it a few moments before serving, in order to undergo a slight cooking process; whereas chopped parsley may be strewn over a dish at the last moment.

It should be remembered that parsley, when quite fresh and used in moderation, is an excellent thing; but, should it have remained too long in the heat, it becomes quite insufferable.

I cannot, therefore, too strongly urge the advisability of using it in the freshest possible state, and it would even be wiser to discard it entirely than to be forced to ignore this condition. (Modern refrigeration keeps it from wilting.)

Parsley Sprigs.—These are chiefly used in garnishing dishes, and it is well for the purpose to make as much use as possible of the curl-leaf kind, after having removed the long stalks. Keep the sprigs in fresh water until required.

Fried Parsley.—This consists of the sprigs, well drained of water after washing, and immersed for an instant in very hot fat. The moment it is fried drain it carefully, salt it, and place it in a clean towel, where it may get rid of any superfluous fat. It is used to dress fried meats.

188—SALT *Sel*

Two kinds of salt are used in cooking, grey, or sea-salt, and rock-salt. Grey-salt is used more especially for Brines and in the preparation of ices, as its grey color does not allow of its being used indiscriminately.

Be this as it may, many prefer it to rock-salt (coarse white culinary salt) for the salting of stock-pots, roasts, and grills. For the last two purposes it is crushed with a rolling pin, without being pounded, and the result should be such that every grain is distinctly perceptible to the touch. This makes it a coarse salt.

This salt, in melting over a roast or a grill, certainly imparts a supplementary flavor to the latter which could not be had with the use of rock-salt. (The white culinary salt.)

Rock-salt.—This is found on the market in the forms of cooking and table-salt. If the kitchen is only supplied with cooking salt, the quantity required for several days should be dried, pounded in the mortar, and passed through a fine sieve; and then put aside in a dry place for use when wanted. Even table-salt, as it reaches one from the grocer, sometimes needs drying and passing through a sieve before being used.

Spiced Salt.—This condiment, which serves an important purpose in the preparation of meat pies and galantines, is obtained from a mixture of one lb. of table salt with three and one-half oz. of spices (181).

This kind of salt should be carefully kept in a very dry place.

(In the United States we have salt which is already prepared and dried finely ground and packed in containers.—Ed.)

189—VARIOUS PANADAS FOR STUFFINGS

Les Panades Diverses pour Farces

Panadas are those preparations which bind the *forcemeats* and which ensure their proper consistency when they are cooked. They are not necessary to every *forcemeat;* for the *mousseline* kind, which are the finest and lightest, do not require them. Nevertheless, they are useful for varying the taste and the uses of *forcemeats,* and I thought it advisable to introduce them here. The reader will thus be able to use either *forcemeats* with a *panada* base or *mousseline* forcemeats; in accordance with the requirements and his resources.

190—BREAD PANADA   *Panade au Pain*

Put one-half lb. of the soft crumb of bread and one-half oz. of salt into one-half pint of boiling milk. When the crumb has absorbed all the milk, place the saucepan over a brisk fire and stir with a spatula until the paste has become so thick it does not cling any longer to the end of the spatula. Turn the contents of the saucepan into a buttered platter, and lightly butter the surface of the *panada* in order to avoid its drying out while it cools.

191—FLOUR PANADA   *Panade à la Farine*

Put into a small saucepan one-half pint of water, a little salt, and two oz. of butter. When the liquid boils add five oz. of sifted flour, stirring over a brisk fire until it reaches the consistency described in the case of bread *panada*. Use the same precautions with regard to cooling.

192—FRANGIPAN PANADA   *Panade à la Frangipan*

Put into a saucepan four oz. of sifted flour, the yolks of four eggs, a little salt, pepper, and nutmeg. Now add by degrees three oz. of melted butter and dilute with one-half pint of boiled milk. Pass through a strainer, stir over the fire until the boil is reached; set to cook for five minutes while gently whisking, and cool as in the preceding cases.

This is a special *forcemeat* for fowl or fish.

193—CHICKEN FORCEMEAT WITH PANADA AND BUTTER
Farce de Volaille à la Panade et au Beurre

Remove the sinews and cut into cubes, one lb. of chicken-meat. Pound or grind finely and add one-third oz. of salt, a little pepper and nutmeg. When the meat is well pounded remove it from the mortar, and place in its stead one-half lb. of very cold *panada* (190). Finely pound this *panada,* and then add one-half lb. of butter, taking care that the two ingredients mix thoroughly. Now put in the chicken-meat, and wield the pestle or spoon vigorously until the whole mass is completely mixed. Finally, add consecutively two whole eggs and the yolks of four, stirring constantly and seeing that each egg is only added when the one preceding it has become perfectly incorporated with the mass. Rub through a sieve, put the *forcemeat* into a bowl, and smooth it with a wooden spoon and chill.

Test the *forcemeat* by *poaching* a small portion of it in salted, boiling water. This test, which is indispensable, permits rectifying the seasoning and the consistency if necessary. If it be found that the *forcemeat* is too light, a little white of egg could be mixed with it; if, on the other hand, it should be too stiff add a little softened butter.

N.B.—By substituting for chicken veal, game, or fish, etc., any kind of forcemeat may be made; for the quantities of the other ingredients remain the same whatever the basic meat may be.

194—CHICKEN FORCEMEAT WITH PANADA AND CREAM
Farce de Volaille à la panade et a la creme

(For Fine Quenelles.)

Finely pound in a mortar or grind fine one lb. of chicken-meat after having removed the sinews, and seasoned with one-quarter oz. of salt, a little pepper and nutmeg.

When the meat has been reduced to a fine paste, add, very gradually, two oz. of white of egg. Finish with seven oz. of Frangipan *panada* (192), and work vigorously with the pestle or spoon until the whole is blended. Strain through a fine sieve, put the *forcemeat* into a pan sufficiently large to permit working it with ease, and place it on ice for a good hour.

This done, stir the *forcemeat* (still on the ice) for a few seconds with a wooden spoon, then add, in small quantities at a time, one pint of cream. At this stage complete the mixture by adding one-half pint of whipped cream. It should then be found to be very white, smooth, and mellow. Test as directed in the preceding recipe, and add a little white of egg if it is too light, and a little cream if it is too stiff.

N.B.—This *forcemeat* may be prepared from all meats, game, or fish.

195—FINE CHICKEN FORCEMEAT, OR "MOUSSELINE"
Farce Fine de Volaille, ou Mousseline

Remove the sinews, trim, and cut into cubes, one lb. of chicken-meat. Season with one oz. of salt, a little pepper and nutmeg.

Finely pound, in mortar or grind and; when it is reduced to a paste, gradually add the whites of two eggs, vigorously working with the pestle or wooden spoon.

Strain through a fine sieve, put the *forcemeat* into a dish, stir it once more with the wooden spoon for a moment or two, and combine with it, gradually, one pint of thick, fresh cream, working with great caution and keeping the receptacle on ice.

Remarks Relative to Mousseline Forcemeat.—This, like the preceding forcemeats, may be prepared from any kind of meat. The addition of the white of egg is not essential if the meats used already possess a certain quantity of albumen; but without the white of egg the *forcemeat* absorbs much less cream.

This *forcemeat* is particularly suited to preparations with a shell-fish base. Incomparable delicate results are obtained by the process, while it also furnishes ideal *quenelles* for the purpose of garnishing soup. In a word, it may be said of *mousseline forcemeat* that, where it can replace all other kinds, none of these can replace it.

N.B.—*Mousseline forcemeats* of all kinds, with meat, poultry, game, fish, or shell-fish, may be made according to the principles and quantities given above.

196—PORK FORCEMEAT FOR VARIOUS USES
Farce de Porc pour Pièces Diverses

Remove the sinews, and cut into large cubes, two lbs. of tender-loin of pork, and the same weight of fresh, fat bacon. Season with one and three-quarter oz. of spiced salt (188), chop the tenderloin and bacon up, together or separately, pound them finely in the mortar or grind, and finish with two eggs and two tablespoons of brandy.

This *forcemeat* is used for ordinary meat pies and *terrines*. Strictly speaking, it is "sausage-meat." The inclusion of eggs in this *force-*

meat really only obtains when it is used to stuff joints that are to be *braised,* such as stuffed breast of veal; or in the case of meat pies and *terrines.* The addition of the egg in these cases prevents the fat from melting too quickly, and thus averts the drying out of the *forcemeat.*

197—FORCEMEAT FOR GALANTINES, PIES, AND TERRINES
Farces pour Galantines, Pâtés, et Terrines

Remove the sinews, and cut into cubes, one lb. of fillet of veal and as much tenderloin of pork; add to these two lbs. of fresh, fat bacon, also cut into cubes. Season with three oz. of spiced salt, chop the three ingredients together or apart, and then finely pound or grind them. Finish with three eggs and three tablespoons of burnt brandy, strain through a sieve, and place in a bowl.

When about to serve this stuffing, add to it a little *fumet* corresponding with the meat that is to constitute the dish. For *terrines,* meat pies, and *galantines* of game, one-quarter or one-fifth of the *forcemeat's* weight of *gratin* stuffing (proper to the game in preparation) is added.

198—VEAL FORCEMEAT WITH FAT, OR GODIVEAU
Farce de Veau à la Graisse, ou Godiveau

Remove the tendons and cut into cubes, one lb. of fillet of veal; also detach the skin and filaments from two lbs. of the very dry fat of beef kidneys. First, chop these up separately, then combine and pound them in the mortar or grind. Season with one-half oz. of salt, a little pepper, some nutmeg, and pound again until the veal and fat become completely mixed. Now add four eggs, consecutively, and at intervals of a few minutes, without ceasing to pound, and taking care to add each egg after the preceding one has been properly mixed with the mass. Spread the *forcemeat* thus prepared on a dish, and put it covered on ice until the next day.

The next day pound once more, and add little by little fourteen oz. of very clean ice (in small pieces); or, instead, an equal weight of iced water, adding this also very gradually.

When the *godiveau* is properly moistened, *poach* a small portion of it in boiling water in order to test its consistency. If it is too firm, add more ice to it; if, on the other hand, it seem too flimsy, add a little of the white of an egg. For the uses of *godiveau* and *quenelles* see No. 205.

199—VEAL FORCEMEAT WITH FAT AND CREAM
Farce de Veau à la Graisse et à la Crême

Chop finely and separately one lb. of very white fillet of veal, with sinews removed, cut into cubes, and one lb. of the fat pared from a beef kidney.

Combine the veal and the fat in the mortar, and pound or grind through chopper until the two ingredients form a fine and even paste. Season with one-half oz. of salt, a little pepper, and some nutmeg, and add consecutively two eggs and two yolks, after the manner of the preceding recipe and without ceasing to pound. Strain through a sieve, spread the forcemeat on a dish, and keep it on ice until the next day.

Next day pound the forcemeat again for a few minutes, and add to it, little by little, one and one-half pints of cream.

Test as before, and rectify if necessary, either by adding cream or by thickening with the white of an egg.

200—CHICKEN FORCEMEAT FOR GALANTINES, PIES, and TERRINES
Farce de Volaille pour Galatines, Pâtés, et Terrines

The exact weight of chicken-meat used as the base of this *forcemeat* determines the quantities of its other ingredients. Thus the weight of meat afforded by a fowl weighing four lbs. is estimated at twenty oz. after deducting the breasts which are always reserved. Hence the quantities for the *forcemeat* are regulated thus:—

Chicken-meat, twenty oz.; lean pork, eight oz.; tenderloin of veal, eight oz.; fresh, fat bacon, thirty oz.; five whole eggs, spiced salt, two oz.; brandy, one-fifth pint.

Chop up, either together or separately, the chicken-meat, the veal, the pork, and the bacon. Put all these into the mortar, pound them very finely with the seasoning, or grind through chopper, add the eggs consecutively, and, last of all, pour in the brandy.

REMARKS

1. The quantity of spiced salt varies, a few grains either way, according as to whether the atmosphere be dry or damp.

2. According to the purpose of the *forcemeat,* and with a view to giving it a finer flavor, one may, subject to the resources at one's disposal, add a little raw trimmings of *foie gras* to it; but the latter must not, in any case, exceed one-fifth of the *forcemeat* in weight.

3. As a rule, *forcemeat* should always be rubbed through a sieve so as to ensure its being fine and even.

4. Whether the *foie gras* is added or not, chicken *forcemeat* may always be completed with two or three oz. of chopped truffles per lb. of its volume, if desired and available.

201—GAME FORCEMEAT FOR PIES AND TERRINES
Farce de Gibier pour Pâtés et Terrines

This follows the same principles as the chicken *forcemeat*, as, the weight of the game-meat determines the quantities of the other ingredients. The proportions are precisely the same amount of veal, pork, bacon, and the seasoning. The procedure is also the same, while the appended remarks likewise apply.

202—GRATIN FORCEMEAT FOR ORDINARY HOT, RAISED PIES
Farce Gratin pour Pâtés Chauds

Put into a saucepan containing one oz. of very hot butter, one-half lb. of fresh, fat bacon, cut into large cubes, brown quickly, and drain.

Quickly brown in the same butter one-half lb. of fillet of veal cut like the bacon and drain in the same way.

Now rapidly brown one-half lb. of pale calf's liver, also cut into large cubes. Put the veal and the bacon back into the saucepan with the liver, add the necessary quantity of salt and pepper, two oz. of mushroom peels, one oz. of truffle peels (raw if possible), chopped shallots, a sprig of thyme, and a small piece of bay leaf. Put the whole on the fire for two minutes, drain the bacon, the veal, and the liver, and put the gravy aside. Stir into and swash the saucepan with one-quarter pint of Madeira.

Pound or grind the bacon, veal, and liver quickly and finely, while adding consecutively six oz. of butter, the yolks of six eggs, the gravy that has been put aside, one-third pint of cold, reduced Espagnole (22), and the Madeira from the pan.

Strain through a sieve, place in a tureen, and smooth with the wooden spoon.

N.B.—To make a *gratin forcemeat* with game, substitute for the veal that game-meat which may happen to be required.

203—PIKE FORCEMEAT FOR QUENELLES LYONNAISE
Farce de Brochet pour Quenelles Lyonnaise

Forcemeats prepared with the flesh of the pike are extremely delicate. Subject to circumstances, they may be prepared according to any one of the three recipes (193, 194, 195). There is another excel\

lent method of preparing this *forcemeat* which I shall submit here, as it is specially used for the preparation of pike *forcemeat* à la Lyonnaise.

Pound in a mortar one lb. of the meat of a pike, without the skin or bones; combine with this one-half lb. of stiff frangipan (192), season with salt and nutmeg, pass through a sieve, and put back into the mortar.

Vigorously work the *forcemeat* in order to make it combine, and gradually add to it one-half lb. melted beef-suet. The whole half-pound, however, need not necessarily be beef-suet; beef-marrow or butter may form part of it in the proportion of half the weight of the beef-suet.

When the *forcemeat* is very fine and smooth, remove it from the mortar and place it in a bowl surrounded with ice until wanted, or keep it in the refrigerator.

204—SPECIAL STUFFINGS FOR FISH   *Farces Spéciales pour Poisson*

These preparations diverge slightly from the *forcemeats* given above, and they are of two kinds. They are used to stuff such fish as mackerel, herring, shad, etc., to which they lend a condimentary touch that makes these fish more agreeable to the taste, and certainly more digestible.

First Method.—Put into a bowl four oz. of raw, chopped *milt*, two oz. of bread-crumbs, steeped in milk and well pressed out, and one and one-half oz. of the following fine herbs, mixed in equal quantities and finely chopped:—Chives, parsley, chervil, shallots, sweet basil, half a garlic clove (crushed), then two whole eggs, salt, pepper, and nutmeg.

Chop up all these ingredients together so as to mix them thoroughly.

Second Method.—Put into a bowl four oz. of bread-crumbs soaked in milk and well pressed out; one-half oz. of onion and one-half oz. of chopped shallots, slightly cooked in butter, and cold; one oz. of fresh mushrooms, chopped and well pressed in a towel; a tablespoon of chopped parsley; a clove of garlic the size of a pea. crushed; salt, pepper, and nutmeg, and two eggs.

Mix it as above.

205—FORCEMEAT BALLS OR QUENELLES   *Quenelles*

Various Ways of Moulding and Poaching.—Whatever be the required size or shape of *quenelles* there are four ways of making them:—(1) By rolling them; (2) by moulding them with a spoon; (3) by forming them with a pastry-bag; (4) by moulding them by hand into the shape of a kidney.

1. *To roll quenelles* it is necessary to keep the *forcemeat* somewhat stiff, and therefore this process could not well apply to the *mousseline* forcemeats. Place one-quarter lb. of *forcemeat,* when ready, on a floured board, and, hands covered with flour, roll the preparation until it has lengthened itself into the form of a sausage, the thickness of which depends upon the required size of the intended *quenelles.*

Cut the sausage of *forcemeat* in slices with a floured knife, and roll each section with the finger-tips until the length it assumes is three times that of its diameter. The balls should be put aside on a floured tray as soon as they are made.

The Poaching of Rolled Quenelles.—When all the *forcemeat* has been used up, the balls are gently tilted into a saucepan containing boiling, salted water, so calculated in quantity to not be too tightly squeezed. The saucepan is covered and kept on the side of the fire until all the balls have risen to the surface and are almost out of the water. They are then lifted out with a skimmer and placed in a bowl of cold water.

At last, when they have properly cooled, they are carefully drained on a cloth and put aside on a dish until required.

When the *quenelles* are needed for immediate use it would be better not to cool them.

2. *To Mould Quenelles with a Spoon.*—This method may be applied to all *forcemeats,* and makes the balls much softer, as the *forcemeat* need not be so stiff. First, butter the saucepan or the tray, on which the balls are to be laid, by means of a brush, and let the butter cool.

Put the saucepan on the table in front of you and a little to the right; on the left, place the saucepan or bowl containing the *forcemeat,* and on the further side of the buttered saucepan there should be a receptacle containing hot water, into which the spoon used for moulding is placed. For ordinary *quenelles* two large teaspoons are used, one of which is kept in the hot water as stated above. Now, with the other held in the left hand, take up a little of the *forcemeat* just enough to fill the spoon); withdraw the second spoon from the hot water and place it, upside down, on the other spoon.

This smooths the top of the *forcemeat.* Now, with the help of the second spoon, remove the whole of the contents of the first spoon.

and overturn the second spoon on the spot in the tray or saucepan which the ball is supposed to occupy. The second spoon, being at once moist and hot, allows the *forcemeat* to leave it quite easily in the shape of a large olive. Renew this operation until the whole of the forcemeat has been used up.

The Poaching of Spoon-moulded Quenelles.—When all the balls have been moulded, place the tray on the side of the stove and pour enough boiling, salted water over them to moisten them abundantly. Leave them to *poach,* and from time to time move and shake the tray or pan; then, when they have swollen sufficiently and seem soft and firm to the touch, drain them. If they are to be used at once they should be placed directly in the sauce. If they have been prepared in advance, it would be well to cool them as directed under rolled *quenelles.*

3. *To Form Quenelles with a Pastry-bag.*—This process is especially recommended for small, fine, and light *forcemeat* balls intended for soup garnish. For, besides being extremely quick, it permits making them in any desirable size or shape.

Butter a tray or a pan, and leave to cool. Put the *forcemeat* into a bag fitted with a tube at its narrowest end. The tube may be grooved or smooth, and its size must be in accordance with that intended for the proposed balls. Now squeeze out the latter, proceeding in the usual way and laying them very closely.

The Poaching of Quenelles made by the above Process, with ordinary or Mousseline Forcemeat.—These *quenelles* are *poached* in exactly the same way as the spoon-moulded ones.

The Poaching of Godiveau Quenelles made with a Pastry-bag.—These quenelles or balls are laid on a piece of fine, buttered paper, which is placed upon a buttered tray. The *godiveau* must not be too stiff, and the balls are laid by means of the pastry-bag side by side and slightly touching one another. When the tray is covered place it in a very moderate oven for a few minutes. The balls are *poached* when a thin condensation of grease may be seen to glisten on their surfaces. On the appearance of this greasy film remove them from the oven and overturn the tray, carefully, upon a marble slab, taking care that the tray does not press at all upon the balls, lest it crush them. When the latter are nearly cold the paper which covers them is taken off with caution, and all that remains to be done is to put them carefully away on a dish until they are wanted.

4. *To Mould Forcemeat with the Fingers.*—This excellent process is as expedient as that of the pastry bag, and it produces beautifully

shaped balls. Place on the edge of a table, in front of you, a saucepan three-quarters full of boiling, salted water, the handle being turned to the opposite side of you. Now take a piece of string one yard in length, double it over, and tie the free ends to a weight of two lbs., letting the two strands twist round each other and hang down.

This done, there should be a loop at the top of the string. Put this loop over the handle of the saucepan, and draw the string diametrically across to you, letting the weight pull the string tightly down on the side opposite to the handle. When this has been done, with the left hand, take some of the *forcemeat*, smoothing it with a spoon, and, placing the spoon near the string with the right, first finger, then take a portion of the preparation about equal to the intended size of the balls. This portion of the *forcemeat* remaining suspended on your first finger, now scrape it across the string, and the ball falls beneath into the saucepan containing the water. When all the stuffing has been moulded in this way the saucepan is placed on the fire to complete the *poaching* of the balls, and the precautions indicated in the preceding processes are observed.

CHAPTER VIII

THE VARIOUS GARNISHES FOR SOUPS

ROYALES

206—ORDINARY ROYALE *Royale Ordinaire*

Put one oz. of chervil into one pint of boiling consommé, cover the saucepan, and let infusion proceed away from the fire for twenty minutes. Now pour this infusion over two eggs and six yolks, beaten briskly in a bowl, and mix with the beater. Strain through muslin, and carefully remove the froth that has formed. Pour into buttered moulds; *poach* in a *bain-marie* (water-bath), as in the case of cream, and take great care that the water in the *bain-marie* does not boil.

According to the way in which the *royale* is to be divided, it may be *poached* either in large or small "Charlotte" (custard) moulds, but the latter, large and small alike, must be well buttered.

If the preparation be put into large moulds, thirty-five or forty minutes should be allowed for *poaching;* if, on the other hand, the moulds are small, about fifteen minutes would suffice.

Always let the *royale* cool in the moulds.

207—DESLIGNAC OR CREAM ROYALE *Deslignac or Royale à la Crème*

Bring to a boil one pint of thin cream, and pour it, little by little, over one egg and six yolks, well beaten in a bowl. Season with a little salt and nutmeg, strain through muslin, and, for the *poaching,* follow the directions given above.

208—CHICKEN ROYALE *Royale de Volaille*

Finely pound three oz. of cooked white chicken-meat, and add three tablespoons of cold Béchamel (28). Put this paste in a bowl, season with a little salt and a dash of nutmeg, dilute with one-fifth pint of cream, and strain through a fine sieve.

Thicken this preparation with one egg and the yolks of three, and *poach* in small or large moulds, in accordance with the procedure already described.

209—GAME ROYALE *Royale de Gibier*

Finely pound or grind three oz. of the cooked meat of game which gives its name to the preparation, and add three tablespoons of cold Espagnole Sauce (22) and one-fifth pint of rich cream, in small quantities at a time. Warm the seasoning with a very little cayenne, strain through a fine sieve, thicken with one egg and three yolks, and *poach* as before.

210—FISH ROYALE *Royale de Poisson*

Stew in butter four oz. of fillet of sole cut into cubes, or the same quantity of any other fish suited to the nature of the intended soup. Cool, pound finely, and add, little by little, two tablespoons of cold Béchamel (28) and one-quarter pint of cream. Season with salt and a pinch of nutmeg, and strain through a fine sieve. Thicken with the yolks of five eggs, and *poach* in large or small moulds.

211—CARROT OR CRECY ROYALE *Royale de Carotte ou Crécy*

Stew gently in butter five oz. of the outside part of carrots. Cool, crush in a mortar or grind and gradually add two tablespoons of Béchamel (28) and one-fifth pint of rich cream. Season with table-salt and a pinch of sugar, and deepen the tint of the *royale* with a few drops of vegetable red coloring. Strain through a fine sieve, thicken with one egg and four yolks, put into moulds, and *poach*.

212—FRESH PEAS OR ST. GERMAIN ROYALE
Royale Saint-Germain de Purée de Pois Frais

Cook one-half lb. of fresh, small peas in boiling water with a bunch of chervil and a few leaves of fresh mint. Pass through a sieve, and dilute the *purée* (in a saucepan) with two-fifths of its volume of the liquor it has been cooked in and one-fifth of cream. Add a little sugar, the necessary salt, one egg, and two yolks. Pass through a fine strainer, and *poach* in well-buttered moulds.

213—VARIOUS ROYALES *Royales Diverses*

Royales may also be made with leeks, celery, etc., the procedure being as follows:—

Finely mince or grind six or seven oz. of the chosen vegetables; stew the same gently and thoroughly in butter, and press through a fine sieve. Add to the resulting *purée* three tablespoons of Béchamel (28), one-fifth pint of cream, two eggs, and four yolks. Put into large or small moulds, and *poach.*

Remarks.—In order that these *royales* may have the required delicacy, I should urge the reader not to exceed the prescribed quantities of eggs and yolks, these being so calculated as to exactly produce the consistency required.

214—THE DIVIDING UP OF ROYALES   *La Division des Royales*

When the *poaching* is done take the mould or moulds out of water, and leave the *royale* to cool in them. Do not turn out the moulds while the preparation is hot, as it would surely separate. It only assumes the necessary solidity for being cut up by means of the cohesion and condensation of its various ingredients during the cooling process.

If the royale has been poached in small moulds, slightly trim the cylinders of *royale,* cut them across into slices, and stamp them uniformly with a plain or fancy cutter.

If the royale has been poached in large moulds, remove it from these, and place it on a napkin; trim the tops, cut into half-inch slices, and stamp with small, fancy cutters of different shapes. These little portions of *royale* must always be stamped very neatly and quite regularly.

215—CHIFFONADE   *Chiffonade*

The name *"Chiffonade"* is given to a mince of sorrel or lettuce, intended as a complement for such soups as "Potage de santé," "le Germiny," etc., or various clear consommés like *"Julienne."*

To prepare *Chiffonade,* first carefully shred the sorrel or lettuce, and remove all the leaf-ribs. Carefully wash the leaves, and squeeze them tightly between the fingers of the left hand and the table top. Now cut them into fine strips with a sharp knife.

If the *Chiffonade* is intended for a consommé, add it to the latter half an hour before serving; it is thus actually cooked in the soup itself. If, as is most often the case, it is intended for a thick soup, it is better to let it melt well in butter, to moisten it with a little consommé, and to let it boil for ten minutes before adding it to the soup.

Whatever the purpose is for which it is made, *chiffonade* should always be prepared with very tender sorrel or lettuce.

216—DIRECTIONS FOR SOUPS WITH PASTES

Potages avec des Croutes

Vermicelli and the various Italian pastes should be used in the proportion of about three oz. per quart of consommé. They should first be thrown into boiling, salted water, where they are left to *poach* for three minutes, then they are drained, cooled, and their cooking is completed in the consomme.

The parboiling of these pastes is necessary in order to get rid of the little flecks of flour which adhere to them, and which would otherwise make the consommé cloudy.

Tapioca, sago, salep (edible orchid root) etc., should also be apportioned at about three oz. per quart. But this is only an average, for the quality of this kind of products varies greatly, and it is best to choose the products of an excellent maker, and, in order to avoid surprises, to abide by that choice.

These products need no parboiling; they are merely sprinkled into the boiling consommé while stirring it, and they are left to cook until the soup is quite clear. The boiling should be gentle, and the scum should be removed as often as it forms.

The time allowed for cooking naturally varies in accordance with the quality of the products, but the absolute transparency of the consommé is an infallible sign of its having been completed.

Brazilian or Japanese pearls are similar to large sago and could be used in the same quantities, but they should *poach* for thirty minutes if required to be very transparent.

217—THREADED EGGS

Oeufs Filés

Beat up three eggs in a bowl, season with salt and pepper, and strain through a sieve. Now pour the eggs through a fine strainer, hold same over a saucepan containing some boiling consommé, and shift it about in such a way as to let the egg fall in threads into the boiling liquid beneath, and thus immediately coagulate. Drain the egg-threads very carefully lest they break and use to garnish clear soups.

218—PROFITEROLLES FOR SOUPS

Profiterolles pour Potages

These consist of little *choux* (puff shells) about the size of a large hazel-nut, stuffed with some kinds of *purée,* such as that of *foie gras* with cream, or of chicken, or of vegetables, etc. Four *profiterolles* should be allowed for each person.

To make *profiterolles,* put a few tablespoons of *"pâte à choux"* (cream puff paste) without sugar (2374) into a pastry-bag fitted with a smooth tube, whose opening should be about one-quarter inch in diameter. Squeeze out portions of the preparation on to a baking sheet, so as to form balls about the size of a small hazel-nut; brush with beaten egg and bake in a moderate oven until a light golden brown.

Do not take the *profiterolles* from the oven until they are quite dry.

CHAPTER IX

219—POTATO CROQUETTES *Croquettes à Pommes*

Cook quickly in salted water two lb. of peeled and quartered potatoes. As soon as they seem soft to the finger, drain them, place them in the front of the oven for a few minutes in order to dry, and then turn them into a sieve lying on a cloth, and press them through without rubbing.

Place the *purée* in a saucepan; season with salt, pepper, and nutmeg; add one oz. of butter, and dry; stirring over a brisk fire until the *purée* becomes a well blended paste.

Take off the fire, complete with the yolks of three eggs, well mixed with the rest, and turn the paste out on to a buttered dish, taking care to spread it in a rather thin layer, so as to hasten its cooling. Butter the surface to prevent drying out.

To make croquettes, equal parts of this paste, portions weighing about one and one-half oz. are rolled on a flour-dusted board into the shape of a cork, a ball, or a patty. These are now dipped into an *Anglaise* (174) and rolled in bread-crumbs or raspings, the latter being well patted on to the surface of the croquettes, lest they should fall into the frying fat. Let the patting also help to finish off the selected shape of the objects. These are then plunged into hot fat, where they should remain until they have acquired a fine, golden color.

220—DAUPHINE POTATOES *Pommes Dauphine*

Prepare as above the required quantity of paste, and add per lb. six oz. of *pâte à choux*, without sugar (2374).

Mix the two pastes thoroughly.

Dauphine potatoes are moulded in the shape of small cylinders, and they are treated *à l'Anglaise*, like the croquettes.

221—DUCHESS POTATOES *Pommes Duchesse*

These are the same as the croquettes, though they are differently treated. They are made on a floured board in the shape of diminutive cottage-loaves, little shuttle-shaped loaves, small patties, and diamonds or rectangles. They are brushed with beaten egg, and when their shape is that of patties, rectangles, or diamonds, they are decorated by means of a small knife.

After this operation, which is to prevent the brushed egg from blistering, they are baked in the oven for a few minutes previous to being used in garnishing the dishes they accompany.

222—MARQUIS POTATOES   *Pommes Marquise*

Take one lb. of croquette paste (219) and add six oz. of very red, thick tomato-*purée* (29). Pour this mixture into a pastry bag fitted with a large, grooved tube, and squeeze it out upon a baking-tray in shapes resembling large meringue shells.

Slightly brush their surfaces with beaten egg and put them into the oven for a few minutes before using them to decorate the dish.

223—ORDINARY OR DRY DUXELLE   *Duxelle Sèche*

The uses of *Duxelle* are legion, and it is prepared thus:—Slightly fry one teaspoon of onions in one tablespoon of butter and oil mixed. Add to this four tablespoons of mushroom stalks and peels, chopped and well pressed in a towel to expel their moisture. Stir over a brisk fire until the latter has completely evaporated; season with salt, pepper, and nutmeg, and one teaspoon of well-chopped parsley, mixing the whole thoroughly.

Transfer to a bowl, cover with a piece of white, buttered paper, and put aside until wanted.

224—DUXELLE FOR STUFFED VEGETABLES
Duxelle pour Légumes Farcis

Put six tablespoons of dry *duxelle* into a small saucepan, and add three tablespoons of half-glaze sauce (23) containing plenty of tomato, crushed garlic the size of a pea, and two tablespoons of white wine. Set to simmer until the required degree of consistency is reached.

N.B.—A tablespoon of fine, fresh bread-crumbs may be added to the *duxelle* in order to thicken it.

225—DUXELLE FOR GARNISHING SMALL PIES, ETC.
Duxelle pour Garnitures Diverses

To four tablespoons of dry *duxelle* add four tablespoons of ordinary pork *forcemeat* (196).

226—MAINTENON PREPARATION USED IN STUFFING
Préparation à la Maintenon

Put one pint of Béchamel (28) into a saucepan with one-half pint of Soubise (104), and reduce to half while stirring over a brisk fire. Thicken, away from the fire, by means of the yolks of five eggs, and add four tablespoons of minced mushrooms, either cooked in the ordinary way or stewed in butter.

227—MATIGNON   *Matignon*

This preparation serves chiefly for covering certain large joints of meat, or fowl, to which it imparts an appropriate flavor. It is made as follows:—Finely mince two medium carrots (the outside part only), two onions, and two stalks of celery taken from the heart. Add one tablespoon of raw lean ham, cut *paysanne*-fashion, a sprig of thyme, and half a bay leaf, crushed.

Stew in butter, and finally stir into the saucepan two tablespoons of Madeira and swash and scrape the pan.

228—MIREPOIX   *Mirepoix*

The purpose of *Mirepoix* in culinary preparations is the same as that of *Matignon,* but its mode of use is different.

Its ingredients are the same as those of the *Matignon,* but instead of being minced they are cut up into more or less fine dice, in accordance with the use for which the preparation is intended.

Instead of the ham, fresh and slightly-salted pork or fresh bacon may be used, while both the ham and the bacon may be excluded under certain circumstances.

229—FINE OR BORDELAISE MIREPOIX   *Mirepoix Bordelaise Fine*

Coarse *Mirepoix,* which are added to certain preparations in order to lend these the proper flavor, are generally made immediately before being used, but this is not so in the case of the finer *Mirepoix,* which chiefly serves as an accompaniment to crayfish and lobsters. This is made in advance, and as follows:—

Cut into dice four oz. of the outside part only of carrots, the same quantity of onion, and one oz. of parsley. In order that the *Mirepoix* may be still finer, these ingredients may now be chopped, but in this case it is advisable to thoroughly press them in a corner of a towel, so as to squeeze out their juice, the mere process of stewing not being sufficient for this purpose.

Should this juice be allowed to remain in the *Mirepoix,* more particularly if it must be kept some time, it would probably give, rise to mustiness or fermentation.

Put the ingredients into a small stewpan with one and one-half oz. of butter and a little powdered thyme and bay leaf, and stew until all is well cooked. This done, turn the preparation out into a small bowl, heap it together with the back of a fork, cover it with a piece of wax paper, and put aside until wanted.

230—VARIOUS SALPICONS   *Salpicons Divers*

Salpicon is a term applied to a number of diced preparations which may be either simple or compound.

Salpicons are simple or compound. Simple if they only contain one product, such as the meat of a fowl, or of game, of beef, *foie gras,* various fish, ham or tongue, mushrooms, truffles, etc. Compound if they consist of two or more of the above-mentioned ingredients which may happen to combine suitably.

The preparatory method consists in cutting the various ingredients into dice.

The series of preparations arises from the many possible combinations of the products, each particular combination bearing its own name.

Thus *Salpicons* may be Royal, Financier, Chasseur, Parisien, Montglas, etc.; of whichever kind, however, *Salpicons* are always mixed with a blending sauce which is in accordance with their purpose and ingredients.

231—BATTER FOR VARIOUS FRITTERS

Pâté à Frire pour Beignets Divers

Put into a bowl one lb. of sifted flour, one-quarter oz. of salt, one tablespoon of oil or melted butter, and the necessary quantity of barely lukewarm water. If the batter is to be used at once mix the ingredients by turning them over and over without stirring with a spoon, for stirring would give the batter an elasticity which would prevent its adhering to immersed solids. Should the batter be prepared beforehand, however, it may be stirred, since it loses its elasticity when left to stand any length of time.

Before using it add the whites of two eggs whisked to a froth.

232—BATTER FOR VEGETABLES   *Pâté à Frire pour Légumes*

Put one lb. of sifted flour into a bowl with one-quarter oz. of salt and two tablespoons of oil or melted butter. Dilute with one egg and the necessary quantity of cold water. Keep this batter somewhat thin, do not stir it, and let it rest for a few hours before using.

233—BATTER FOR FRUIT AND FLOWER FRITTERS
            Pâté à Frire pour Beignets de Fruits et de Fleurs

Put one lb. of flour into a bowl with one-quarter oz. of salt and two tablespoons of oil or melted butter. Dilute gradually with one-quarter pint of beer and a little tepid water.

When about to use the batter mix in the whites of two eggs whisked to a froth.

N.B.—Keep this batter thin, if anything, and above all do not stir too much.

234—BATTER FOR OVEN-GLAZED FRUIT FRITTERS
            Pâté à Frire pour Beignets Glacés au Four

Mix one lb. of flour with two tablespoons of oil, a few grains of salt, two eggs (added one after the other), the necessary quantity of water, and one oz. of sugar. Keep this preparation in a lukewarm place to let it ferment, and stir it with a wooden spoon before using it to cover the food.

Remarks.—Batter for fruit fritters may contain a few tablespoons of brandy, in which case an equal quantity of the water must be eliminated.

235—PREPARATION FOR STUFFING CUTLETS A LA PROVENCALE
            Préparations pour Farce Provençale

Put one pint of Béchamel (28) into a saucepan and reduce it until it has become quite thick. Add the yolks of four eggs, and finish it away from the fire with a crushed piece of garlic as large as a pea, and one-quarter lb. of grated cheese.

236—THE PREPARATION OF SOUPS *Préparation des Potages*

The nutritious liquids known under the name of Soups are of comparatively recent origin. Indeed, as they are now served, they do not date any further back than the early years of the nineteenth century.

The soups of old cookery were, really, complete dishes, wherein the meats and vegetables used in their preparation were assembled. They, moreover, suffered from the effects of the general confusion which reigned in the menus of those days. These menus seem to have depended in no wise, for their items, upon the progressive satisfaction of the diner's appetites, and a long procession of dishes was far more characteristic of the meal than their judicious order and diversity.

In this respect, as in so many others, Carême was the reformer, and, if he were not, strictly speaking, the actual initiator of the changes which ushered in our present methods, he certainly had a large share in the establishment of the new theories.

Nevertheless, it took his followers almost a century to bring soups to the perfection of to-day, for modern cookery has replaced those stodgy dishes of yore by comparatively simple and savory preparations which are veritable wonders of delicacy and taste. Now, my attention has been called to the desirability of drawing up some sort of classification of soups, if only with the view of obviating the absurdity of placing such preparations as are indiscriminately called *Bisque, Purée, Cullis,* or Cream under the same head. Logically, each preparation should have its own special formula, and it is impossible to admit that one and the same can apply to all.

It is generally admitted that the terms *Veloutés* and *Creams,* whose introduction into the vocabulary of cookery is comparatively recent, are peculiarly well suited to supplant those of *Bisque* and *Cullis,* which are steadily becoming obsolete, as well as that too vulgar term *Purée*. Considerations of this kind naturally led me to a new classification of soups, and this I shall disclose later.

I shall not make any lengthy attempt here to refute the arguments of certain autocrats of the dinner-table who, not so many years ago, urged the total abolition of soups. I shall only submit to their notice the following quotation from Grimod de la Reynière, one of our most illustrious gastronomists: "Soup is to a dinner what the porch or gateway is to a building," that is to say, it must not only form the first portion thereof, but it must be so devised as to convey some idea of the whole to which it belongs; or, after the manner of an overture in a light opera, it should divulge what is to be the dominant phrase of the melody throughout.

I am at one with Grimod in this, and believe that soups have come to stay. Of all the items on a menu, soup is that which exacts the most delicate perfection and the strictest attention, for upon the first impression it gives to the diner the success of the latter part of the meal largely depends.

Soups should be served as hot as possible in very warm plates or cups, especially in the case of consommés when these have been preceded by cold hors-d'œuvres.

Hors-d'œuvres are pointless in a dinner, and even when oysters stand as such they should only be allowed at meals which include no soup.

Those hors-d'œuvres which consist of various fish, smoked or in oil, and strongly seasoned salads, leave a disagreeable taste on the diner's palate and make the soup which follows seem flat and insipid if the latter be not served boiling hot.

CLASSIFICATION OF SOUPS

This includes (1) clear soups, (2) thick soups, (3) special soups of various kinds, (4) classical vegetable soups, including some local preparations.

237—CLEAR SOUPS   *Les Potages Clairs*

Clear soups, of whatever nature the base may be, whether meat, poultry, game, fish, shell-fish, or turtle, etc., are made according to one method only. They are always clear consommés to which has been added a slight garnish in keeping with the nature of the consommé.

238—THICK SOUPS *Les Potages Liés*

These are divided into three leading classes as follows:—(1) The *Purées, Cullises,* or *Bisques.* (2) Various *Veloutés.* (3) Various Creams.

Remarks.—Though the three preparations of the first class are practically the same, and, generally speaking, the *Cullises* and the *Bisques* may be considered as *purées* of fowl, game, or shell-fish, it is advisable to distinguish one from another by giving each a special name of its own.

Thus the word *purée* is most suitably applied to any preparation with a vegetable base. The term *Cullis* or *Coulis* is best fitted to preparations having either poultry, game, or fish for base, while *bisque,* in spite of the fact that in former days it was applied indiscriminately to *purées* of shell-fish, poultry, pigeons, etc., distinctly denotes a *purée* of shell-fish (either lobster, crayfish, or shrimp, etc.).

In short, it is imperative to avoid all confusion and to give everything its proper name, or, at least, that name which identifies it most correctly.

239—PUREES *Les Purées*

Starchy vegetables, such as dried beans and lentils, and the mealy ones, such as the potato, need no additional thickening ingredient, since the flour or *fecula* which they contain amply suffices for the binding of their *purées.*

On the other hand, succulent vegetables like carrots, pumpkins, turnips, celery, etc., and herbs cannot dispense with a thickening ingredient, as their *purées* of themselves do not hold together and bind.

Binding or Thickening Elements; Quantities.—In order to effect the binding of vegetable *purées,* either rice, potato, or soft crumb of bread cut into dice and fried in butter may be used.

The proportion of these per pound of vegetables should be respectively three oz., ten oz., and ten oz. Soft bread dice, prepared as described above, were greatly used in old cookery, and they lend a mellowness to a *purée* which is quite peculiar to them.

The Dilution of Purées.—Generally this is done by means of ordinary white consommé, though in certain cases, as, for instance, if the soup is a *Lenten* one, milk is used.

The Finishing.—When the *purées* have been strained and brought to the required consistency they should be boiled and stirred. Then they are placed on the side of the fire to simmer for twenty-five or thirty minutes. It is at this stage that they are purified by means of the careful removal of all the scum that forms on their surface.

When ready to serve complete them, away from the fire, with three oz. of butter per quart of soup, and pass them once more through a strainer.

Purée Garnishes.—These are usually either small fried crusts, small dice of potato fried in butter, a *chiffonade,* some kind of little *brunoise,* or, more generally, chervil *pluches.*

240—CULLISES *Les Coulis*

Cullises have for their base either poultry, game, or fish.

The thickening ingredients used are:—

For fowl, two or three oz. of rice, or three-quarters pint of poultry *velouté* (26) per lb. of fowl.

For game, three or four oz. of lentils, or three-quarters pint of game Espagnole (22) per lb. of game.

For fish, a clear *panada* made of French bread soaked in boiling salted milk. Use five oz. of bread and one good pint of milk per lb. of fish. Having strained and made up the *Cullises,* boil them while stirring (except in the case of fish *cullises,* which must not boil, and must be served as soon as they are made), then place them in a *bain-marie* (water-bath) and butter their surfaces lest a skin should form.

At the last moment complete them with two or three oz. of butter per quart.

The garnish of poultry or game *cullises* consists of either small dice of game or fowl breasts, which should be kept aside for the purpose; a fine *julienne* of these uncooked breasts, or small *quenelles* made from them.

The garnish of fish *cullis* is generally fish-fillets *poached* in butter and cut up into small dice or in *julienne*-fashion.

241—BISQUES *Les Bisques*

The invariable base of *Bisques* is shell-fish cooked in *mirepoix.*

Their thickening ingredients may be rice, fish *velouté,* or crusts of bread fried in butter, the proportion being three oz. of rice, ten oz. of bread-crusts, or three-quarters pint of fish *velouté* (26a) per lb. of shell-fish cooked in *mirepoix* (228).

When the soup is strained, treat it in precisely the same way as the *cullises.*

The garnish consists of small dice of the meat from the shell-fish used. These pieces should be put aside from the first.

242—THE VELOUTES   *Les Veloutés*

These differ from the *purées, cullises,* and *bisques* in that their invariable thickening element is a *velouté* whose preparation is in harmony with the nature of the ingredients of the soup, these being either vegetables, poultry, game, fish, or shell-fish.

The Preparation of the Velouté.—Allow three and one-half oz. of white *roux* per quart of the diluting liquid. This liquid should be ordinary consommé for a *velouté* of vegetables or herbs, chicken consommé for a poultry *velouté,* or very clear fish fumet for a fish or shell-fish *velouté.* The procedure is exactly the same as that described under (25) of the leading sauces.

The Apportionment of the Ingredients.—In general, the quantities of each ingredient are in the following proportion:—*Velouté,* one-half; the *purée* of the substance which characterizes the soup, one-quarter; the consommé used to bring the soup to its proper consistency, one-quarter. In respect of finishing ingredients, use, for thickening, the yolks of three eggs and one-fifth pint of cream per quart of soup.

Thus for four quarts of poultry *velouté* we arrive at the following quantities:—

Poultry *velouté,* three pints; *purée* of fowl obtained from a cleaned and drawn hen weighing about three lbs., one quart; consommé for regulating consistency, one quart; binding, twelve egg yolks and four-fifths pint of cream.

Rules Relative to the Preparation.—If the *velouté* is to be of lettuce, chicory, celery, or mixed herbs, these ingredients are scalded for five minutes, drained, gently stewed in butter, and added to the prepared *velouté* in which their cooking is completed.

If carrots, turnips, onions, etc., are to be treated, finely mince them, stew them in butter without allowing them to acquire any color, and add them to the *velouté.*

If fowl be the base, cook it in the *velouté.* This done, withdraw it, remove the meat, finely pound or grind, and add it to the *velouté,* which is then rubbed through a fine sieve.

In the case of fish the procedure is the same as for fowl. For game, roast or *sauté* the selected piece, bone it, finely pound or grind the meat, and combine the latter with the *velouté,* which should then be rubbed through a fine sieve.

For shell-fish, cook these in a *mirepoix,* finely pound them together with the latter, add to the *velouté,* and pass the whole through a fine sieve.

The Completing of Velouté.—Having passed the soup through a fine sieve, bring it to its proper degree of consistency with the necessary quantity of consommé, boil while stirring, and place in a *bain-marie* or water-bath.

At the last moment finish the soup with the binding and two oz. of butter per quart of liquid.

Garnish for Velouté.—In the case of vegetables: *Chiffonade,* fine *printaniers,* or *brunoise.*

For fowl and game: The breasts of one or the other, *poached* and cut into small dice or in *julienne*-fashion; little *quenelles* made with the raw breasts, or either fowl or game royales (208).

For fish: Small dice or fine *julienne* of fish fillets *poached* in butter.

For shell-fish: Small dice of cooked shell-fish meat put aside for the purpose.

Remarks.—In certain cases these garnishes are increased by means of three tablespoons of *poached* rice per quart of the soup.

243—THE CREAMS   *Les Crèmes*

Practically speaking, the preparation of the creams is the same as that of the *veloutés,* but for the following exceptions:—

1. In all cases, whatever be the nature of the soup, *velouté* is substituted for clear Béchamel.

2. The correct consistency of the soup is made by means of milk instead of consommé.

3. Creams do not require egg-yolk bindings.

4. They are not buttered, but they are finished with one-fifth or two-fifths pint of fresh cream per quart.

Creams permit the same garnishes as the *veloutés.*

244—SPECIAL SOUPS AND THICKENED CONSOMMES
Les Potages Spéciaux et les Consommés Liés

These are of different kinds, though their preparation remains the same, and they do not lend themselves to the requirements of *veloutés* ·or creams. I should quote as types of this class the Ambassador, à l'Américaine, Darblay, Faubonne, etc.

The same holds good with thickened consommés, such as "Germiny," "Coquelin," etc.

245—VEGETABLE SOUPS   *Les Potages à Légumes*

These soups, of which the *"Paysanne"* (peasant type) is the radical type, do not demand very great precision in the apportionment of the vegetables of which they are composed; but they need great care and attention, notwithstanding.

The vegetables, in the majority of cases, must undergo a long stewing in butter, an operation the object of which is to expel their vegetable juice and to saturate them with butter.

In respect of others which have a local character, the vegetables should be cooked with the liquid, without a preparatory stewing.

246—FOREIGN SOUPS   *Potages Etrangères*

In the course of Part II of this book* I shall refer to certain soups which have a foreign origin, and whose use, although it may not be general, is yet sufficiently common. If only for the sake of novelty or variety, it is occasionally permissible to poach upon the preserves of foreign nations; but apart from this there exist among the recipes of foreigners many which can but enrich their adopter, besides being generally appreciated.

Braising, Poaching, Sautés, and Poëles

Except for the roasts, grills, and fryings, which will be discussed later, all culinary operations dealing with meat are related to one of the four following methods: *Braising, poëles, poaching,* and *sautés.*

These four methods of cooking belong, however to the sauces, and this explains how it is that the latter hold such a pre-eminent position in French cookery.

Before devoting any attention to particular recipes, which will be given in the second part of this work, it seemed desirable to me to recapitulate in a general way the theory of each of these cooking methods. These theories are of paramount importance, since it is only with a complete knowledge of them that good results may be obtained by the chef or cook.

247—ORDINARY BRAISINGS   *Les Braises Ordinaires*

Of all the various culinary operations, *braisings* are the most expensive and the most difficult. Long and assiduous practice alone can teach the many difficulties that this mode of procedure entails, for it is one which demands extraordinary care and the most constant attention. Over and above the question of care and that of the quality of meat used, which latter consideration is neither more nor less important here than in any other cooking operation, there are also these conditions to be fulfilled in order that a good

*A. Escoffier, *The Escoffier Cook Book* (New York: Crown Publishers, Inc., 1941).

braising may be obtained, namely, that excellent stock should be used in moistening, and that the *braising* base be well prepared.

Meats that are Braised.—Mutton and beef are *braised* in the ordinary way, but veal, lamb, and poultry are *braised* in a manner which I shall treat of later.

Meat intended for *braising* need not, as in the case of roasts, be that of young beasts. The best for the purpose is that derived from an animal of three to six years of age in the case of beef, and one to two years in the case of mutton. Good meat is rarely procured from animals more advanced than these in years, and, even so, should it be used, it would not only be necessary to lengthen the time of cooking a great deal, but the resulting food would probably be fibrous and dry.

Properly speaking, meat derived from old or ill-nourished beasts only answers two purposes in cookery, the preparation of consommés and that of various kinds of stock.

The Larding of Meats for Braising.—When the meat to be *braised* is ribs or fillet of beef, it is always *interlarded,* and consequently never dry if of good quality. But this is not the case with the meat of the rumps, or with leg of mutton. These meats are not sufficiently fat of themselves to allow for prolonged cooking without becoming dry. For this reason they are *larded* with square strips of bacon fat, which should be the length of the meat under treatment, and about half an inch thick. These strips of fat are first seasoned with pepper, nutmeg, and spices, sprinkled with chopped parsley, and then *marinated* for two hours in a little brandy. They should be inserted into the meat at equal distances apart by means of special larding needles. The proportion of fat to the meat should be about three oz. per lb.

To Marinate Braisings.—Larded or not, the meats intended for *braising* gain considerably from being *marinated* for a few hours in the wines which are to supply their moistening and the *aromatics* (herbs and vegetables) constituting the base of their liquor. Before doing this season them with salt, pepper, and spices, rolling them over and over in these in order that they may absorb the seasoning thoroughly. Then place them in a receptacle just large enough to contain them, between two beds of prepared vegetables and herbs, which will be detailed hereafter; cover them with the wine which forms part of their *braising*-liquor, and which is generally a white or red "vin ordinaire," in the proportion of one-quarter pint per lb.

of meat, and leave them to *marinate* for about six hours, taking care to turn them over three or four times during that period.

The Aromatics or Base of the Braising.—These are thickly sliced and fried carrots and onions, in the proportion of one oz. per lb. of meat, one herb bunch (176), including one garlic clove and one and one-half oz. of fresh, *blanched* bacon-rind.

To Fry, Prepare, and Cook Braised Meat.—Having sufficiently *marinated* the meat, drain it on a sieve for half an hour, and wipe it dry with a clean piece of linen. Heat some clarified fat skimmed from white consommé (2) in a thick saucepan of convenient size, or a braising-pan, and when it is sufficiently hot put the meat in the saucepan and let it brown on all sides. The object of this operation is to cause a contraction of the pores of the meat, thereby surrounding the meat with a kind of crust, which prevents the inner juices from escaping too soon and converting the braising into a boiling process. The frying should, therefore, be a short or lengthy process according to whether the amount of meat to be braised be small or large.

Having properly fried the meat, remove it from the braising-pan, cover it with slices of larding-bacon if it be lean, and tie it. In the case of fillets and ribs of beef, this treatment may be dispensed with, as they are sufficiently well supplied with their own fat.

Now pour the *marinade* prepared for the meat into the braising-pan, and place the meat on a bed composed of the vegetables the *marinade* contained. Cover the pan and rapidly reduce the wine. When this has assumed the consistency of syrup add sufficient brown stock (7) to cover the meat (it being understood that the meat only just conveniently fills the pan), cover the braising-pan, set to boil, and then put it in a moderate oven. Let the meat cook until it may be deeply pricked with a testing needle without any blood being drawn. At this stage the first phase of *braising,* of which the theory shall be given after, comes to an end, and the meat is transferred to another clean utensil just large enough to hold it.

With respect to the cooking liquor, either of the two following modes of procedure may now be adopted:—

1. If the liquor is required to be clear it need only be strained, over the meat, through muslin, while the braising-pan should be placed in the oven, where the cooking may go on until completed, interrupting it only from time to time in order to baste the meat. This done, thicken the liquor with arrowroot or flour, after the manner of an ordinary thickened gravy (41).

2. If, on the contrary, a sauce be required, the liquor should be reduced to half before being put back on the meat, and it is restored to its former volume by means of two-thirds of its quantity of Espagnole sauce (7) and one-third of tomato *purée*, or an equivalent quantity of fresh tomatoes.

The cooking of the meat is completed in this sauce, and the basting should be carried on as before. When it is cooked—that is to say, when the point of a knife may easily be thrust into it without meeting with any resistance whatsoever—it should be carefully withdrawn from the sauce; the latter should be again strained through muslin and then left to rest, with a view to letting the grease settle on the surface.

Carefully remove this grease, and rectify the sauce with a little excellent stock if it is too thick, or by reduction if it is too thin.

The Glazing of Braised Meat.—*Braised* meat is *glazed* in order to make it more appetizing, but this operation is by no means essential, and it is quite useless when the meat is cut up previous to being served.

To *glaze* meat place it as soon as cooked in the front of the oven, sprinkle it slightly with its cooking liquor (gravy or sauce), and put it into the oven so that this liquor may dry. Being very gelatinous, the latter adheres to the meat, while its superfluous water evaporates, and thus coats the solid with a thin film of meat-*glaze*. This operation is renewed eight or ten times, whereupon the meat is taken from the oven, placed on a dish, and covered until it is served.

Various Remarks relative to Braising.—When a braised meat is to be accompanied by vegetables, as in the case of beef à la mode, these vegetables may either be cooked with the meat during the second *braising* phase, after they have been duly browned in butter with a little salt and sugar, or they may be cooked separately with a portion of the *braising*-liquor. The first procedure is the better, but it lends itself less to a correct final dressing. It is, therefore, the cook's business to decide according to circumstances which is the more suitable of the two.

I pointed out above that the cooking of *braised* meat consists of two phases, and I shall now proceed to discuss each of these, so that the reader may thoroughly understand their processes.

It has been seen that meat, to be *braised*, must in the first place be browned all over, and this more particularly when it is very thick. The object of this operation is to hold in the meat's juices, which would otherwise escape from the cut surfaces. Now, this searing produces a kind of protective coating around the flesh, which gradually thickens during the cooking process until it reaches the center. Under the influence of the heat of the surrounding liquor the meat fibres contract, and steadily drive the contained juices towards the center. Soon the heat reaches the center, where, after having effected a change in the juices therein collected, the latter release the superfluous water they contain. This water quickly vaporizes, and by so doing distends and separates the tissues surrounding it. Thus, during this first phase, a concentration of juices takes place in the center of the meat. It will now be seen that they undergo an absolutely different process in the second.

As shown, the disintegration of the muscular tissue begins in the center of the meat as soon as the temperature which reaches there is sufficiently intense to vaporize the collected juices. The tension of the vapor given off by the latter increases by less resistance; it therefore exerts considerable pressure upon the tissues, though now its direction is the reverse of what it was in the first place, from the center to the outside surface.

Gradually the tissues relax under the pressure and the effects of cooking, and, the work of disintegration having gradually reached the browned surface, the latter also relaxes in its turn and allows the constrained juices to escape and to mix with the sauce. At the same time, however, the latter begins to filter through the meat, and this it does in accordance with a well-known physical law, namely, capillarity. This stage of the *braising* demands the most attentive care. The *braising*-liquor is found to be considerably reduced and no longer covers the meat, for the operation is nearing its end. The bared meat would, therefore, dry very quickly, if care were not taken to baste it constantly and to turn it over and over, so that the whole of the muscular tissue is moistened and thoroughly saturated with the sauce. By this means the meat acquires that mellowness which is typical of *braisings* and distinguishes them from other preparations.

I should be loath to dismiss this subject before pointing out two practices in the cooking of braisings which are as common as they are absolutely wrong. The first of these is the *"pinçage"* of the braising base. Instead of laying the fried meat on a bed of *aromatics* (vegetables and herbs), likewise fried beforehand, many cooks place the meat, which they often fail to brown, on raw *aromatics* at the bottom of the braising-pan. The whole is sprinkled with a little melted fat, and the *aromatics* are left to fry, on one side only, until they begin to burn on the bottom of the receptacle.

If this operation were properly conducted it might be tolerated, even though *aromatics* which are only fried on one side cannot exude the same savor as those which are fried all over. But nine times out of ten the frying is too lengthy a process; from neglect or absent-mindedness the *aromatics* are left to burn on the bottom of the pan, and there results a bitterness which pervades and spoils the whole sauce.

As a matter of fact, this process of *"pinçage"* is an absurd carica-ture of a method of preparing *braisings* which was very common in old cookery, the custom of which was not to prepare the *braising*-liquor in advance, but to cook it and its ingredients simultaneously with the meat to be *braised*. This method, though excellent, was very expensive, the meats forming the base of the *braising*-liquor consist-ing of thick slices of raw ham or veal. The observance of economy, therefore, long ago compelled cooks to abandon this procedure. But routine has perpetuated the form of the latter without insisting upon the use of its ingredients, which were undoubtedly its essential part. Routine has even, in certain cases, aggravated the first error by instituting a habit consisting of substituting bones for the meats formerly employed—an obviously ridiculous practice.

In the production of ordinary consommé (1) we saw that bones, even when taken from veal, as is customary in the case of *braising*-liquor, require, at the very least, ten to twelve hours of cooking before they can yield all their soluble properties. As a proof of this it is interesting to note that, if bones undergo only five or six hours of cooking, and are moistened again and cooked for a further six hours, the liquor of the second cooking yields more meat-*glaze* than that of the first; though it must be admitted that, while the latter is more gelatinous, it has less savor. But this gelatinous property of bones is no less useful to *braisings* than is their savor, since it is the former that supplies the mellowness, which nothing can replace and without which the sauce can have no quality.

Since, therefore, the longest time that a *braising* can cook is from four to five hours, it follows that, if bones be added, their properties will scarcely have begun disintegrating when the meat is cooked. They will, in fact, have yielded but an infinitesimal portion of these properties; wherefore their addition to the *braising* is, to say the least, quite useless.

It now remains to be proved that the above method is bad from another point of view.

I suppose I need not fear contradiction when I assert that, in order that a *braising* may be good, its sauce should be short and correspondingly substantial; also that the sauce obtained from a piece of meat moistened with a quart of liquid cannot be so good as that resulting from the moistening of a pint only.

It is more particularly on this account that I advise a braising utensil which can only just hold the meat, for since, in the first stage, the meat is only moistened with the *braising*-liquor, the smaller the receptacle may be the less liquor will it require, and the latter will in consequence be the tastier. Hence, if bones be added to the *braising*, the utensils must necessarily be larger, and a greater quantity of *braising*-liquor must be used. But this liquor will not be nearly so savory as that obtained from the process I recommend; in fact, it will be but a rather strong broth, quite unfit for the impregnation of the meat, and the final result will be a tasteless lump of fibre instead of a succulent *braising*.

I must apologize to the reader for my insistence with regard to these questions, but their importance is such that success is beyond reach in the matter of brown sauces and *braisings* unless the above details have been thoroughly grasped. Moreover, the explanations given will afford considerable help in the understanding of operations which I shall give later; therefore it is to be hoped that the examination of the theories involved, however long this has been, will prove of use and assistance.

248—BRAISING OF WHITE MEATS   *Les Braises de Viandes Blanches*

The braising of white meats as it is now effected in modern cookery is, strictly speaking, not *braising* at all, inasmuch as the cooking is stopped at the close of the first of the two phases which I mentioned when discussing brown *braisings*. True, old cookery did not understand *braising* in the way that the modern school does, and under the ancient régime large pieces, especially of veal, were frequently cooked until they could almost be scooped out with a spoon. This practice has been generally, though mistakenly, shunned, but its name survives.

White *braisings* are made with the neck, the saddle, the loin, the fillets, the *fricandeaus,* and the sweet-bread of veal, young turkeys and fat pullets, and sometimes, though less frequently, *relevés* of lamb, hindquarters or saddle. The procedure is the same for all these meats; the time of cooking alone varies in accordance with their size. The *aromatics* are the same as those of the brown *braisings,* but the frying of them is optional.

The moistening liquor is brown veal stock (9).

Mode of Procedure.—Except for the veal sweet-breads, which are always *blanched* before being *braised,* the meats or poultry to be treated may always be slightly cooked and browned in butter, on all sides. This is not essential in all cases, but I think that when they do undergo something of the kind they dry less quickly. Now place them in a utensil just large enough to hold them and deep enough to keep the lid from touching them. Place the *aromatics* under them and moisten with a little veal stock (9); set to boil on a moderate fire, and reduce the veal stock with the lid on. When this stock has assumed the consistence of a *glaze,* add a further similar quantity of fresh stock, and reduce as before. The third time moisten the veal until it is half covered, and put the pan into a moderate oven.

The meat needs constant basting while it cooks, in order to avoid its drying; and, as the stock is very gelatinous, it forms a coating on the surface which resists the evaporation of the contained juices; for these, being insufficiently constrained by the slight browning the meat has undergone, tend to vaporize under the influence of the heat.

It is for this reason that the stock must be reduced to a *glaze* before finally moistening. If the moistening were all done at once, the liquor would not be sufficiently dense to form the coating mentioned, and the meat would consequently dry on being set to cook.

Braised white meat is known to be cooked when, after having deeply pricked it with a testing needle, it exudes an absolutely colorless liquid. This liquid denotes that the meat is cooked to the center, and as a result the blood has decomposed.

There lies the great difference between brown *braisings* and white-meat *braisings.* The latter are practically roasts, and they should not be made with any but young poultry or meats, very fat and tender, for they cannot go beyond their correct time of cooking, which equals that of roasts, without immediately losing all their quality. A quarter of an hour too much in the cooking of a roast of veal weighing about six lbs. is enough to make the meat dry and unpalatable, and to thoroughly spoil it, whereas a brown *braising* cannot be over-cooked, provided it does not burn.

White *braised* meats are generally *glazed,* and this process is especially recommended for larded pieces, which, though less common nowadays than formerly, can still claim many advantages

249—POACHINGS   *Les Pochés*

However nonsensical it may sound, the best possible definition of a *poaching* is a boiling that does not boil. The term *poach* is extended to all slow processes of cooking which involve the use of a liquor, however small. Thus the term *poach* applies to the cooking in *court-bouillon* of large pieces of turbot and salmon, as well as to fillets of sole cooked with a little fish *fumet*, to hot *mousselines* and *mousses*, cooked in moulds, to *quenelles* which are cooked in salted water, to eggs announced as *"poached,"* to creams, various *royales*, etc. It will readily be seen that among so many different products, the time allowed for the cooking in each case must differ sometimes widely from the rest. The treatment of them all, however, is subject to this unalterable principle, namely, that the *poaching* liquor must not boil, though it should reach a degree of heat as approximate as possible to the boiling-point. Another principle is that large pieces of fish or poultry be set to boil in cold liquor, after which the latter is brought to the required temperature as rapidly as possible. The case may be the same with fillets of sole, or poultry, which are *poached* almost dry; but all other preparations whose mode of cooking is *poaching* gain by being immersed in liquor which has reached the required temperature beforehand.

Having regard to the many forms and kinds of products that are *poached*, it would be somewhat difficult to state here the details and peculiarities proper to each in the matter of *poaching*; I think, therefore, I should do better to leave these details to the respective recipes of each product, though it will now be necessary to disclose the way of *poaching* poultry, if only with a view to thoroughly acquainting the reader with the theory propounded above.

Properly prepare the piece of poultry to be *poached*, and truss it with its legs folded back alongside of the breast.

If it is to be stuffed, this should be done before trussing.

If it is to be *larded* or *studded*, either with truffles, ham, or tongue, rub it when trussed on the breasts and legs with half a lemon, and dip the same portions of its body (namely, those to be *larded* or *studded*) for a few moments in boiling white stock (10). The object of this operation is to slightly stiffen the skin, thus facilitating the *larding* or *studding*.

The Cooking of the Piece of Poultry.—Having stuffed, *larded*, or *studded* it, if necessary, and having, in any case, trussed it, place it in a receptacle just large enough to hold it, and moisten with some excellent white stock previously prepared.

Set to boil, skim, put the lid on, and continue the cooking at a low simmer. It is useless to work too quickly, as the cooking would not be shortened a second by so doing. The only results would be:—

1. Too violent evaporation, which would reduce the liquor and disturb its transparency.

2. The running of a considerable risk of bursting the piece of poultry, especially when the latter is stuffed.

The fowl, or whatever it may be, is known to be cooked when, after pricking the thick of the leg close to the "drumstick," the oozing liquid is white.

Remarks.—(*a*) The need of *poaching* poultry in a receptacle just large enough to hold the bird is accounted for as follows: (1) The piece must be wholly immersed in the stock during the cooking process. (2) As the liquor used is afterwards served as an accompanying sauce to the dish, the less there is of it the more saturated does it become with the juices of the meat, and, consequently, the better it is.

(*b*) (1) The white stock used in *poaching* should be prepared beforehand, and be very clear.

(2) If the poultry were set to cook with the products constituting the stock, even if these were more than liberally apportioned, the result would be bad, for inasmuch as a fowl, for example, can only take one and one-half hours, at the most, to cook, and the time required for extracting the nutritious and flavoring principles from the ingredients of the stock would be at least six hours, it follows that the fowl would be cooking in little more than hot water, and the resulting sauce would be quite devoid of savor.

250—POELES   *Les Poêlés*

Poêlés are, practically speaking, roasts, for the cooking periods of each are the same, except that the former are cooked entirely or almost entirely with butter. They represent a simplified process of old cookery, which consisted in enveloping the object to be treated, after frying it, in a thick coating of *Matignon*. It was then wrapped with thin slices of pork fat, covered with buttered paper, placed in the oven or on a spit, and basted with melted butter while it cooked. This done, its grease was drained away, and the vegetables of the *Matignon* were put in the braising-pan wherein the piece had cooked, or in a saucepan, and were moistened with excellent Madeira or highly seasoned stock. Then, when the liquor had thoroughly absorbed the aroma of the vegetables, it was strained, and its grease was removed just before serving. This excellent method is worthy of continued use in the case of large pieces of poultry.

Preparation of Poëléd Meats.—Place in the bottom of a deep and thick receptacle, just large enough to hold the piece to be poëléd, a layer of raw *Matignon* (227). The meat or poultry is placed on the vegetables after it has been well seasoned, and is copiously sprinkled with melted butter; cover the pan, and put it into an oven whose heat is not too hot. Set it to cook gently in this way, after the manner of a stew, and frequently sprinkle with melted butter.

When the meats or the pieces of poultry are cooked, the pan is uncovered so that the former may brown; then they are transferred to a dish which should be kept covered until taken to the table. Now add to the vegetables (which must not be burned) a sufficient quantity of brown veal stock (9), transparent and highly seasoned; set the whole to boil gently for ten minutes, strain through a napkin, carefully remove all grease from the *poëléd* stock and send it to the table in a sauceboat at the same time as the meat or poultry, which, by the way, is generally garnished.

Remarks on Poëlés.—It is of paramount importance that these be not moistened during the process of cooking, for in that case their savor would be the same as that of *braised* white meats.

Nevertheless, an exception may be made in the case of such game birds as pheasants, partridges, and quails, to which is added, when nearly cooked, a small quantity of burnt brandy.

It is also very important that the vegetables should not have their grease removed before their moistening stock is added to them. The butter used in the cooking absorbs a large proportion of the savor of both the vegetables and the meat which is being cooked, and, to make good this loss, it is essential that the moistening stock remain at least ten minutes in contact with the butter. At the end of this time it may be removed without in the least impairing the aroma of the stock.

Special Poëlés known as "En Casserole," or "En Cocotte."—The preparations of meats, of poultry, or game, known as *"en casserole"* or *"en cocotte,"* are actual poëlés cooked in special earthenware utensils and served in the same. Generally, preparations known as *"en casserole"* are simply cooked in butter, without the addition of vegetables.

When the cooking is done, the piece being prepared is removed for a moment, and some excellent brown veal stock (9) is poured

into the pan. This is left to simmer for a few minutes; the superfluous butter is then removed; the piece is returned to the earthenware utensil, and it is kept hot, without being allowed to boil, until
it is served.

For preparations termed *"en cocotte,"* the procedure is the same,
except that the piece is garnished with such vegetables as mushrooms, the hearts of artichokes, small onions, carrots, turnips, etc.,
which are either cut out or pared, and half cooked in butter before
being used.

One should endeavor to use only fresh vegetables, and these
should be added to the meat constituting the dish in such a way
as to complete their cooking with it.

The earthenware utensils used for this purpose improve with
use, provided they be cleaned with clean, fresh water, without any
soda or soap. If new utensils have to be used, these should be filled
with water, which is set to boil, and they should then undergo at
least twelve hours' soaking. For the prescribed time this water
should be kept gently boiling, and then the utensil should be well
wiped and soaked again, in fresh water, before being used.

251—THE SAUTES   *Les Sautés*

What characterizes the process we call *"sauté"* is that the object
treated is cooked dry—that is to say, solely by means of a fatty
substance such as butter, oil, or grease.

Sautés are made with cut-up fowl or game, or with meat suitably
divided up for the purpose.

All products treated in this way must be frizzled—that is to say,
they must be put into the fat when it is very hot in order that a
hardened coating may form on their surfaces which will keep their
juices in. This is more particularly desirable for red meats such
as beef and mutton.

The cooking of fowl *sautés* must, after the meats have been seared,
be completed on the stove or, with lid off, in the oven, where they
should be basted with butter after the manner of a roast:

The pieces are withdrawn from the cooking utensil with a view
to swashing and scraping it, after which, if they be put back into
the sauce or accompanying garnish, they should only remain therein
a few moments or just sufficiently long to become properly warm.

The procedure is the same for game *sautés*.

Sautés of red meats, such as tournedos, kernels, cutlets, fillets, and noisettes, are always made on the stove; the meats are quickly browned and cooked with a small quantity of clarified butter.

The thinner and smaller they are, the more rapidly should the searing process be done.

When blood appears on the surface of their uncooked side, they should be turned over; when drops of blood begin to gather on their other side, they are known to be cooked.

The swashing or swirling of the .pan happens in all *sautés*. After having removed the treated product from the saucepan, remove the grease and pour the flavoring liquid (a wine), that forms part of the accompanying sauce, into the saucepan.

Set to boil and scrape the pan, so that the solidified gravy lying on the bottom may dissolve, and add the sauce; or simply add the flavoring liquid to the prepared sauce or accompanying garnish of the *sauté*. The utensil used must always be just large enough to hold the objects to be cooked. If it be too large, the parts left uncovered by the cooked meats burn, and swashing is then impossible, whence there results a loss of the solidified gravy which is an important ingredient in the sauce.

Sautés of white meats, such as veal and lamb, must also be quickly browned in hot fat, but their cooking must be completed gently on the side of the fire, and in many cases with the lid on.

Preparations of a mixed nature, which partly resemble *sautés* and partly *braisings,* are also called *sautés*. Stews, however, is their most suitable name.

These dishes are made from beef, veal, lamb, game, etc., and they are to be found in Part II under the headings Estouffade; Goulash; Sautés: Chasseur, Marengo, Bourgeoise; Navarin; Civet; etc.

In the first stage of their preparation, the meats are cut up small and fried like those of the *sautés;* in the second, slow cooking with sauce or garnish makes them similar to *braised* meats.

ROASTS, GRILLS, FRYINGS

Roasts

OF the two usual methods of roasting, the spit will always be used in preference to the oven, if only on account of the conditions under which the cooking is done, and whatever be the kind of fuel used—wood, coal, gas or electricity.

The reason of this preference is clear if it be remembered that, in spite of every possible precaution during the progress of an oven roast, it is impossible to avoid an accumulation of vapor around the cooking object in a closed oven. And this steam is more particularly objectionable inasmuch as it is excessive in the case of delicately flavored meats, which are almost if not entirely impaired thereby.

The spitted roast, on the contrary, cooks in the open in a dry atmosphere, and by this means retains its own peculiar flavor. Hence the unquestionable superiority of spitted roasts over the oven kind, especially in respect of small game birds.

In certain circumstances and places there is no choice of methods, and, like it or not, the oven has to be used; but, in this case at least, all possible precautions should be observed in order to counteract the effects of the steam above mentioned.

252—LARDING BACON FOR ROASTS   *Lardons pour Larder les Viandes*

Poultry and game to be roasted ought generally to be partly covered with a large thin slice of larding bacon, except those pieces of game which in special cases are *larded*.

The object and use of these slices is not only to shield the breasts of fowl and game from the severe heat of the fire, but also to prevent these from drying, while the legs, which the heat takes much longer to penetrate than the other parts, are cooking. The slices of bacon should therefore completely cover the breasts of fowl and game, and they should be tied on to the latter by means of string.

In some cases roasts of meat are covered with layers of veal- or beef-fat, the object of which is similar to that of the bacon mentioned above.

253—SPITTED ROASTS   *Les Rôtis en Broche*

The whole theory of roasts on the spit might be condensed as follows:—

In the case of meat, calculate the intensity of the heat used according to the cut to be roasted, the latter's size and quality, and the time it has hung. Experience, however, is the best guide, for any theory, whatever be its exactness, can only give the leading principles and general rules, and cannot pretend to supply the place of the practised eye and the accuracy which are the result of experience alone.

Nevertheless, I do not say with Brillat Savarin that a good roaster is born and not made; I merely state that one may become a good roaster with application, observation, care, and a little aptitude.

The three following rules will be found to cover all the necessary directions for spitted roasts:—

1. All red meats containing a large quantity of juice should be properly set or browned, and then, according to their size, made to undergo the action of a fire capable of radiating a very penetrating heat with little or no flame.

2. In the case of white meats, whose cooking should be thorough, the fire ought to be so regulated as to allow the roast to cook and brown simultaneously.

3. With small game the fuel should be wood, but whatever fuel be used the fire ought to be burning in such a way as to produce more flame than glowing embers.

254—OVEN ROASTS   *Les Rôtis au Four*

The degree of heat used for each roast must be regulated according to the nature and size of the latter after the manner of spitted roasts.

An oven roast, in the first place, should always be placed on a meat rack or trivet, and this should be of such a height that at no given moment during the cooking process the meat may come in contact with the juices and fat which have drained from it into the utensil beneath. Lacking proper equipment, a spit resting upon the edges of the pan may be used.

No liquid of any kind, gravy or water, need be put in the pan. The addition of any liquid is rather detrimental, since by producing vapor which hangs over the roast it transforms the latter into a stew.

Remarks.—Whether spitted or in the oven, a roast must always be frequently basted with a fatty substance, but never with any other liquid.

255—THE GRAVY OF ROASTS   *Le Fonds de Braise*

The real and most natural gravy for roasts is made from the swashing and scraping (Fr. *deglaçage*) of the baking or dripping-pan, even if water is used as the liquid, since the contents of these utensils represent a portion of the essential principles of the roast fallen from it in the process of cooking. But to obtain this result neither the utensils nor the gravy ought to have burned; the latter should merely have solidified, and for this reason a roast cooked in a very hot oven ought to be laid in a pan only just large enough to hold it, so that the fat may not burn.

The swashing and scraping can in any case only produce a very small quantity of gravy, consequently, when it happens that a greater quantity is required, the need is met beforehand by preparing a stock made from bones and trimmings of a similar nature to the roast for which the gravy is required. The procedure for this is as follows:—

Place the bones and trimmings in a pan with a little fat and literally roast them. Then transfer them to a saucepan, moisten so as to cover with tepid, slightly-salted water, and add the residue of the pan where they were roasted. Boil, skim, and set to cook gently for three or four hours, according to the nature of the products used. This done, almost entirely remove the grease, strain through muslin, and put aside for the purpose of swashing the dripping or baking-pan of the roast.

Swashing and Scraping.—Having removed the roast from the spit or oven, take off a portion of the grease from the baking or dripping-pan, scrape the sides and bottom, and pour into it the required quantity of prepared gravy. Reduce the whole by half, strain through muslin, and almost entirely remove grease.

It is a mistake to remove all the grease from, and to clarify, the gravy of roasts. Treated thus they are certainly clearer and more sightly, but a large proportion of their savor is lost, and it should be borne in mind that the gravy of a roast is not a consommé.

In the matter of roast game birds, the accompanying gravy is supplied by the swashing of the utensil, either with water or a small quantity of brandy. This is a certain means of obtaining a gravy whose savor is precisely that of the game; but occasionally veal gravy is used, as its flavor is neutral, and it therefore cannot impair the particular flavor of the reduced game gravy lying on the bottom of the utensil. The use of stock prepared from the bones and trimmings of game similar to that constituting the dish is also common.

256—THE DRESSING AND ACCOMPANIMENTS OF ROASTS
Le Dressage et les Garnitures des Rôtis

As a rule, a roast ought not to wait. It ought only to leave the spit or oven in order to be served. All roasts should be placed on very hot dishes, slightly sprinkled with fresh butter, and surrounded by bunches of watercress (this is optional). The gravy is invariably served separately.

Roasts of meat and poultry are served as simply as possible.

Small roasted game may be set on fried slices of bread covered with *gratin* stuffing (202).

When lemons accompany a roast, they should be served separately. Pieces of lemon that have once served to garnish a dish must not be used again, for they have mostly been tainted by grease.

The mediæval custom of serving game with the plumage has been abandoned.

Roast game birds *à l'anglaise* are served with or without potato chips, and the three accompaniments are gravy, bread-crumbs, and bread-sauce, particularly in England.

In northern countries game roasts are always accompanied either by slightly sugared stewed apples, or by cherry or apricot jam or currant jelly.

257—GRILLS   *Les Grillades*

Those culinary preparations effected by means of grilling belong to the order called cooking by concentration. And, indeed, in almost all cases, the great object of these operations, I might even say the greatest object, is the concentration, in the center, of the juices and *essences* which represent, most essentially, the nutritive principles of the products cooked.

A grill, which is, in short, but a roast on an open fire, stands, in my opinion, as the remote starting-point, the very genesis of our art.

It was the primæval notion of our forefathers' infantile brains; it was progress born of an instinctive desire to eat with greater pleasure; and it was the first culinary method ever employed.

A little later, and following naturally, as it were, upon this first attempt, the spit was born of the grill; gradually, intelligence supplanted rude instinct; reason began to deduce effects from supposed causes; and thus cooking was launched forth upon that highroad along which it has not yet ceased steadily to advance.

Fuel for Grills.—That mostly used, and certainly the best for the purpose, is live coal or small pieces of charcoal. Whatever fuel be used, however, it is essential that it produce no smoke, even though the grill fire be ventilated by powerful blowers which draw the smoke off. More especially is this necessary, though I admit the contingency is rare, when artificial ventilation has to be effected owing to the fire's burning in the open without the usual help of systematic draughts; for if smoke occasioned by foreign substances or by the falling of the fat itself on to the glowing embers were not immediately carried away, either artificially or by a convenient draught, the grills would most surely acquire a very disagreeable taste.

The Bed of Charcoal.—The arrangement of the bed of charcoal under the grill is of some importance, and it must not only be regulated according to the size and kind of the products to be grilled, but also in such a way as to allow for the production of more or less heat under given circumstances.

The bed should therefore be set in equal layers in the center, but varying in thickness according to whether the fire has to be more or less high and fierce; it should also be slightly raised on those sides which are in contact with the air, in order that the whole burning surface may radiate equal degrees of heat.

The grill must always be placed over the glowing fuel in advance, and it should be very hot when the objects to be grilled are placed upon it, otherwise they would stick to the bars, and would probably be spoiled when turned.

(In the United States the finest grilling equipment is sold for gas, electricity and charcoal which makes the method much easier.—Ed.)

GRILLS CLASSIFIED

Grills may be divided into four classes, of which each demands particular care. They are: (1) Red-meat grills (beef and mutton); (2) White-meat grills (veal, lamb, poultry); (3) Fish; (4) Grills coated with butter and bread-crumbs.

258—RED MEAT GRILLS   *Grillades de Viandes Noires*

I submit as a principle that the golden rule in grills is to strictly observe the correct degree of heat which is proper to each treated food, never forgetting that the larger and richer in nutrition the piece of meat, the quicker and more thorough must be its initial setting.

I have already explained, under *braisings,* the part played by, and the use of, *rissoling* or searing; but it is necessary to revert to this question and its bearing upon grills.

If large pieces of meat (beef or mutton) are in question, the better their quality and the richer they are in juices, the more resisting must be the *rissoled* coating they receive. The pressure of the contained juices upon the *rissoled* coating of this meat will be proportionately great or small according to whether the latter be rich or poor, and this pressure will gradually increase with the rising heat.

If the grill fire be so regulated as to ensure the progressive penetration of heat into the cooking object, this is what happens:—

The heat, striking that surface of the meat which is in direct contact with the fire, penetrates the tissues, and spreads through the layers of meat, driving the latter's juices in front of it. When these reach the opposite, *rissoled,* or seared side of the meat, they are checked, and thereupon, absorbing the incoming heat, effect the cooking of the inner parts.

Of course, if the piece of meat being cooked is very thick, the heat of the fire should be proportionately lessened the moment the initial process of *rissoling* or searing of the meat's surface has been done, the object being to allow the heat to penetrate the cooking body more regularly. If the high temperature of the fire were maintained, the *rissoled* coating on the meat would probably char, and the resulting thickness of carbon would so successfully resist the passage of any heat into the interior that, in the end, while the meat would probably be found to be completely burnt on the outside, the inside would be quite raw.

If somewhat thinner pieces are in question, a quick *rissoling* of their surfaces over a hot fire, and a few minutes of subsequent cooking, will be all they need. No alteration in the intensity of the fire need be sought in this case.

Examples.—A rumpsteak or Châteaubriand (1076), in order to be properly cooked, should first have its outside surface *rissoled* on a very hot fire with a view to preserving its juices, after which cooking may proceed over a moderate fire so as to allow the gradual penetration of the heat into the center of the steak.

Small pieces such as tournedos, small fillets, noisettes, chops, may, after the preliminary process of *rissoling,* or searing, be cooked over the same degree of heat as cooked the outside, because the thickness of meat to be penetrated is less.

The Care of Grills while Cooking.—Before placing the meats on the grill, baste them slightly with clarified butter (175), and repeat this operation frequently during the cooking process, so as to avoid the possible drying of the *rissoled* surfaces.

Grilled red meat should always be turned by means of special tongs, and great care should be observed that its surface is not torn or pierced, lest the object of the preliminary precautions be defeated, and the contained juices escape.

Time of Cooking.—This, in the case of red meats, is arrived at by the following test: if, on touching the meat with one's finger,

it resists any pressure, it is sufficiently cooked: if it gives, it is clear that in the center, at least, it is still rare. The most certain sign, however, that cooking has been completed is the appearance of little beads of blood upon the *rissoled* surface of the meat.

259—WHITE MEAT GRILLS   *Grillades de Viandes Blanches*
That superficial *rissoling* or searing which is so necessary in the case of red meats is not at all so in the case of white, for in the latter there can be no question of the concentration of juices, since these are only present in the form of albumen—that is to say, in the form of juices "in the making," so to speak, which is peculiar to veal and lamb.

For this kind of grills keep a moderate fire, so that the cooking and browning of the meat may take place simultaneously.

White meat grills should be fairly often basted by means of a brush, with clarified butter (175), while cooking, lest their outside dries.

They are known to be cooked when the juice issuing from them is quite white.

260—FISH GRILLS   *Poissons Grillés*
Use a moderate fire with these, and only grill after having copiously sprinkled them with clarified butter (175) or oil. Sprinkle them again while cooking.

A grilled fish is cooked when the bones are easily separated from the meat. Except for the fatty kind, such as mackerel, gray mullet, or herrings, always roll fish to be grilled in flour before sprinkling them with melted butter. The object of so doing is to give them a golden crust, which, besides making them more pleasing, keeps them from drying.

261—THE GRILLING OF PRODUCTS COATED WITH BUTTER AND
    BREAD CRUMBS   *Grillades d'Eléments Panés*
These grills generally consist of only small objects; they must be cooked on a very moderate fire, with the view of enabling them to cook and acquire brown simultaneously. They should also be frequently sprinkled with clarified butter (175), and turned with care, so as not to break their coating, the object of which is to withhold their contained juices.

262—FRYINGS   *Les Fritures*
Frying is one of the principal cooking processes, for the number of preparations that are accomplished by this means is very consid-

erable. Its procedure is governed by stringent laws and rules which it is best not to break, lest the double danger of failure and impairment of material be the result.

The former is easily averted if one is familiar with the process, and pays proper attention to it, while the latter is obviated by precautions which have every *raison d'être,* and the neglect of which only leads to trouble.

The question of the kind of utensil to employ is not so immaterial as some would think, for very often accidents result from the mere disregard of the importance of this matter.

Very often imprudence and excitement on the part of the cook may be the cause of imperfections, the greatest care being needed in the handling of utensils containing overheated fat.

Utensils used in frying should be made of copper, or other resisting metal; they should be in one piece, oval or round in shape, and sufficiently large and deep to allow, while only half-filled with fat, the food being properly cooked by it. The necessity of this condition is obvious, seeing that if the utensil contain too much fat the slightest jerking of it on the stove would spill some of the liquid, and the cook would probably be badly burnt.

Finally, utensils with vertical sides are preferable to those of the slanting kind; more especially is this so in large kitchens where, the work involving much frying, enormous receptacles are required.

(In the United States the finest utensils for frying have been created of stainless metal and the most heat retaining alloys. Both for ordinary and deep fat frying the chef and the household cook alike find utensils to suit their needs and the danger of spilling fat, etc., is eliminated to the greatest degree.—Ed.)

263—FRYING FAT—ITS PREPARATION   *La Graisse pour Fritures*

Any animal or vegetable fat is suitable for frying, provided it be quite pure and possesses a resisting force allowing it to reach a very high temperature without burning. But for frying on a large scale, the use of drippings and clarified fats, such as the fat skimmed from the *"pot-au-feu"* and roasts, should be avoided.

A frying medium is only perfect when it is able to meet the demands of an extended operation, and consists of fresh or raw fats, chosen with care and thoroughly purified by cooking.

Under no circumstances may butter be used for frying on a large scale; even when thoroughly purified, it can only reach a comparatively low degree of heat. It may be used only for small, occasional fryings.

The fat of beef kidney generally forms the base of the grease intended for frying on a large scale. It is preferable to all others on account of its cheapness and the great length of time it can be used, provided it receives the proper care.

Veal-fat yields a finer frying medium, but its resistance is small, and it must, moreover, always be mixed with the beef-fat.

Mutton-fat should be deliberately discarded, for, if it happen to be that of an old animal, it smells of tallow, and, if it is that of a young one, it causes the hot grease to foam and to overflow down the sides of the utensil, this leading to serious accidents.

Pork-fat (lard) is also used for frying, either alone, or combined with some other kind.

In brief, the fat of beef kidney is that which is best suited to frying on a large scale. Ordinary household frying, which does not demand a very resisting grease, may well be effected by means of the above, combined with an equal quantity of veal-fat, or a mixture composed of the fat of beef kidney, veal, and pork in the proportions of one-half, one-quarter, and one-quarter respectively.

The grease used for frying ought not only to be melted down, but also thoroughly cooked, so that it may be quite pure. If insufficiently cooked, it foams on first being used, and so demands all kinds of extra precautions, which only cease to be necessary when constant heating at last rectifies it. Moreover, if it is not quite pure, it easily penetrates immersed solids and makes them indigestible.

All fat used in frying should first be cut into pieces and then put into the saucepan with one pint of water per every ten lbs.

The object of the water is to assist in the melting, and this it does by filtering into the fat, vaporizing, and thereby causing the latter to swell. So long as the water has not completely evaporated, the grease only undergoes the action of liquefaction, the dissolution of its molecules; but its thorough cooking process, ending with its purification, only begins when all the water is gone.

The grease is cooked when the membranes which enveloped it alone remain intact and are converted into cracklings; it gives off smoke which has a distinct smell.

At this stage it has reached such a high temperature that it is best to remove it from the fire for about ten minutes, so that it may cool; then it must be strained through a sieve, or a coarse towel, which must be tightly twisted.

264—THE VARIOUS DEGREES OF HEAT REACHED BY THE FRYING MEDIUM, AND THEIR APPLICATION

Degrés de la Friture et leur Application

The temperature reached by a frying medium depends upon the fat's components and its purity. The various degrees may be classified as moderately hot, hot, very hot.

The expression "boiling hot" is unsuitable, seeing that fat never boils. Butter (an occasional frying medium) cannot go over 248° F. without burning, whereas if it be thoroughly purified it can attain from 269° to 275° F.—a temperature which is clearly below what would be needed for work on a large scale.

Animal fats used in ordinary frying reach from 275° to 284° F. when moderately hot, 320° F. when hot, and 356° F. when very hot; in the last case they smoke slightly.

Pork-fat (lard), when used alone, reaches 392° F. without burning. Very pure goose dripping withstands 428° F.; and, finally, vegetable fats may reach, without burning, 482° F. in the case of cocoa-nut butter, 518° F. with ordinary oils, and 554° in the case of olive oil.

The temperature of ordinary frying fat may be tested thus: it is moderately hot when, after throwing a sprig of parsley or a crust of bread into it, it begins to bubble immediately; it is hot if it crackles when a slightly moist object is dropped into it; it is very hot when it gives off a thin white smoke perceptible to the smell.

The first temperature, "moderately hot," is used for all products containing vegetable water the complete evaporation of which is necessary; for fish whose volume exacts a cooking process by means of penetration, previous to that with concentration.

In the first degree of heat with which it is used the frying fat therefore only effects a kind of preparatory operation.

The second temperature, "hot," is used for all products which have previously undergone an initial cooking process in the first temperature, either for evaporation or penetration, and its object is either to finish them or to cover them with a crisp coating.

It is also applicable to those products upon which the frying fat must act immediately by concentration—that is to say, by forming a set coating around them which prevents the escape of the contained substances.

Objects treated with this temperature are: all those *panés à l'anglaise* or covered with batter, such as various croquettes, *cromesquis,* cutlets, and collops à la Villeroy, fritters of all kinds, fried creams, etc.

In this case the frying medium acts by setting, which in certain cases is exceedingly necessary.

1. If the objects in question are *panés à l'anglaise* (dipped in beaten eggs and rolled in bread-crumbs), the sudden contact of the hot grease converts this coating of egg and bread-crumbs into a resisting crust, which prevents the escape of the substances and the liquefied sauce contained within.

If these objects were plunged in a fat that was not sufficiently hot, the coating of egg and bread-crumbs would not only absorb the frying medium, but it would run the risk of breaking, thereby allowing the escape of the very substances it was intended to withhold.

2. The same holds with objects treated with batter. Hence the absolute necessity of ensuring that setting which means that the covering of batter solidifies immediately. As the substances constituting these various dishes are cooked in advance, it follows that their second heating and the browning of the coating (egg and bread-crumbs or batter) take place at the same time and in a few minutes.

The third temperature, "very hot," is used for all objects that need a quick and firm setting; for all small objects the setting of which is of supreme importance, and whose cooking is affected in a few minutes, as in the case of whitebait.

265—FRYING MEDIUM FOR FISH   *Fritures pour Poisson*

Every frying medium, used for work on a large scale, which has acquired a too decided coloring through repeated use, may serve in the preparation of fish even until its whole strength is exhausted.

Oil is best suited to the frying of fish, especially the very small kind, owing to the tremendous heat it can withstand without burning, for this heat guarantees that setting which is so indispensable.

Except in this case, however, the temperature of the frying medium should be regulated strictly in accordance with the size of the fish to be fried, in order that its cooking and browning may be done simultaneously.

Except whitebait, which is simply rolled in flour, fish to be fried are previously soaked in slightly salted milk and then rolled in flour. From this combination of milk and flour there results a crisp coating which holds those particular principles that the fish exude while cooking.

When finished, fried fish are drained, dried, slightly salted, and served on a napkin or on paper, with a garnish of fried parsley-sprigs and sections of grooved lemon.

266—THE QUANTITY OF THE FRYING MEDIUM
La Quantité de Friture à Employer

This should always be in proportion to the quantity or size of the foods to be fried, bearing in mind that these must always be entirely submerged.

Without necessarily exaggerating, the quantity should invariably be rather in excess of the requirements, and for this reason, the greater the amount of fat, the higher will be the temperature reached, and the less need one fear a sudden cooling of the fat when the objects to be treated are immersed. This sudden cooling is often the cause of great trouble, unless one be working over a fire of such intensity that the fat can return in a few seconds to the temperature it was at before the food were immersed.

267—THE CARE OF THE FRYING MEDIUM
Soins à Donner aux Fritures

Every time the frying fat is used it should, after having been melted, be strained through a towel, for the majority of foods which it has served to cook must have left some particles behind them which might prove injurious to the foods that are to follow.

Objects that are breaded always leave a residue, for instance, which in time assume the form of black powder, while those that have been treated with flour likewise drop some of their coating, which, in accumulating, produces a muddy deposit on the bottom of the utensil.

Not only do these foreign substances disturb the clearness of the fat and render it liable to burn, but they are exceedingly detrimental to the objects that are fried in it later.

Therefore, always strain the fat whenever it is used—in the first place because the proper treatment of the foods demands it, and, secondly, because its very existence as a serviceable medium depends upon this measure.

268—GRATINS   *Les Gratins*

This culinary operation plays a sufficiently important part in the work to warrant my detailing at least its leading points.

The various kinds of the order "Gratins" are (1) the **Complete** *Gratin;* (2) the Rapid *Gratin;* (3) the Light *Gratin;* (4) *Glazing,* which is a form of Rapid *Gratin.*

269—COMPLETE GRATIN   *Le Gratin Complet*

This is the first example of the series; it is that whose preparation is longest and most tiresome; for its principal ingredient, whatever this is, must be completely cooked. Its cooking must moreover be coincident with the reduction of the sauce, which is the base of the *gratin,* and with the formation of the *gratin* proper, the crisp crust which forms on the surface and is the result of the combination of the sauce with the raspings (crumbs) and the butter, under the direct influence of the heat.

In the preparation of complete *gratin,* two things must be taken into account:—The nature and size of the food to be treated, and the degree of heat which must be used in order that the cooking of the food, the reduction of the sauce, and the formation of the *gratin* may be done simultaneously.

The base of complete *gratin* is almost invariably ordinary or *Lenten duxelle* sauce (223), in accordance with the requirements.

The object to be treated with the *gratin* is laid on a buttered dish, surrounded with slices of fresh mushrooms and chopped shallots, and covered with *duxelle* sauce (223). The surface is then sprinkled with raspings (178), and copiously moistened with melted butter. Should the piece be large, the amount of sauce used will be proportionately greater, and the reverse, of course, applies to medium or smaller sizes.

Take note of the following remarks in the making of complete *gratins:*—

1. If too much sauce were used in proportion to the size of the food, the latter would cook and the *gratin* form before the sauce could reach the correct degree of consistency by means of reduction. Hence it would be necessary to reduce the sauce still further on the stove, and thereby give rise to steam which would soften the coating of the *gratin.*

2. If the sauce used were insufficient, it would be reduced before the cooking of the object had been effected, and, more sauce having to be added, the resulting *gratin* would be uneven.

3. The larger the piece, and consequently the longer it takes to cook, the more moderate should be the heat used. Respectively, the smaller it is, the hotter should the fire be.

When taking the *gratin* from the oven squeeze a few drops of lemon-juice over it, and sprinkle it with chopped parsley.

270—RAPID GRATIN   *Le Gratin Rapide*

Proceed as above, with *duxelle* sauce (223), but the foods treated with it, meats, fish, or vegetables, are always cooked and warmed in advance. All that is required, therefore, is to effect the formation of the *gratin* as quickly as possible.

To do this, cover the food under treatment with the necessary quantity of salt, sprinkle with raspings (crumbs) and butter, and set the *gratin* to form in a very hot oven.

271—LIGHT GRATIN   *Le Gratin Léger*

This is proper to use for starchy products, such as macaroni, lazagnes, noodles, gnocchi (dumplings), and consists of a combination of grated cheese, bread-crumbs, and butter. In this case, again, the only end in view is the formation of the *gratin* coating, which must be evenly browned, and is the result of the cheese melting. A moderate heat is all that is wanted for this kind of *gratin*.

Also considered as light *gratins* are those which serve as the complement of stuffed vegetables such as tomatoes, mushrooms, egg-plant, and cucumber, etc. With these the *gratin* is composed of bread-crumbs sprinkled with butter or oil, and it is placed in a more or less intense heat according to whether the vegetables have already been cooked or partially cooked, or are quite raw.

272—GLAZINGS   *Les Glaçages*

These are of two kinds—they either consist of a heavily buttered sauce, or they form from a sprinkling of cheese upon the sauce with which the food to be glazed is covered.

In the first case, after having poured sauce over the food to be treated, place the dish on another dish containing a little water. This is to prevent the sauce separating and boiling. The greater the quantity of butter used, the more intense will be the heat required, in order that a slight golden film may form almost instantaneously.

In the second case, the sauce used is always a Mornay (91). Cover the food in preparation with the sauce, sprinkle with grated cheese and melted butter, and place in fairly intense heat, so that a slight golden crust may form almost immediately, this crust being the result of the combined cheese and butter.

273—BLANCHINGS *Blanchissages*

The essentially unsuitable term *blanchings* is applied in the culinary technology of France to three classes of operations which entirely differ one from the other in the end they have in view.

1. The *blanching* of meats.
2. The *blanching,* or, better, the parboiling of certain vegetables.
3. The *blanching* of certain other vegetables, which in reality amounts to a process of cooking.

The blanching of meats obtains mostly in the case of calf's head and feet and the sweet-breads of veal, sheeps' and lambs' shanks, and lamb's sweet-bread. These meats are first set to soak in cold, running water until they have got rid of the blood with which they are naturally saturated. They are then placed on the fire in a saucepan containing enough cold water to abundantly cover them, and the water is gradually brought to the boil.

For calf's head or feet, boiling may last for fifteen or twenty minutes; veal sweet-breads must not boil for more than ten or twelve minutes; while lamb sweet-breads are withdrawn the moment the boil is reached.

As soon as *blanched,* the meats are cooled in plenty of fresh water before undergoing their final treatment.

The blanching of cocks' combs is exceptional in this, namely, that after the combs have been cleansed of blood—that is to say, soaked in cold water, they are placed on the fire in cold water, the temperature of which must be carefully kept below 113° F. When this degree is approached, take the saucepan off the fire and rub each comb with a cloth, dusted with table-salt, in order to remove the skins; then cool the combs with fresh water before cooking them.

Many people use the *blanching* process with meats intended for "blanquette" or "fricassée." I regard this procedure as quite erroneous, as also the preliminary soaking in cold water.

If the meats or pieces of poultry intended for the above-mentioned preparations be of a good quality (and no others should be used), they need only be set to cook in cold water, or cold stock, and gradually brought to the boil, being stirred repeatedly. The scum formed should be carefully removed, and, in this way, perfectly white meats and stock, with all their savor, are obtained.

As to meats or pieces of poultry of an inferior quality, no soaking and no *blanching* can make good their defects. Whichever way they are treated they remain dry, gray, and savorless. It is therefore simpler and better to use only the finest quality products.

An excellent proof of the futility of soaking and *blanching* meats intended for "fricassées" and "blanquettes" lies in the fact that these very meats, if of good quality, are always perfectly white when they are *braised, poëléd,* or roasted, notwithstanding the fact that these three operations are less calculated to preserve their whiteness than the kind of treatment they are subjected to in the case of "blanquettes" and "fricassées."

Mere routine alone can account for this practice of soaking and *blanching* meats—a practice that is absolutely condemned by common sense.

The term *blanching* is wrongly applied to the cooking of green vegetables, such as string beans, green peas, Brussels sprouts, spinach, etc. The cooking of these, which is effected by means of boiling salted water, ought really to be termed *à l'anglaise.* All the details of the procedure, however, will be given when I deal with the vegetables to which the latter apply.

Lastly, under the name of *blanching,* there exists another operation which consists in partly cooking certain vegetables in plenty of water, in order to rid them of any bitter or pungent flavor they may possess. The time allowed for this *blanching* varies according to the age of the vegetables, but when the latter are young and in season, it amounts to little more than a mere scalding.

Blanching is chiefly resorted to for lettuce, chicory, endives, celery, artichokes, cabbages, and the green vegetables; carrots, turnips, and small onions when they are out of season. In respect of squash, cucumbers, and chayotes, *blanching* is often left to the definite cooking process, which should then come under the head of the *à l'anglaise* cooking.

After the process of *blanching,* the vegetables I have just enumerated are always cooled—that is to say, steeped in cold water until they are barely lukewarm. They are then left to drain through a sieve, previous to undergoing the final cooking process to which they are best suited, this generally being *braising.*

VEGETABLES AND GARNISHES

Various Preparations

274—THE TREATMENT OF DRY VEGETABLES
Préparation des Légumes Secs

It is wrong to soak dried vegetables. If they are of good quality, and the produce of the year, they need only be put into a saucepan with enough cold water to completely cover them, and with one oz. of salt per five quarts of water.

Set to boil gently, skim, add the seasoning, quartered carrots, onions, with or without garlic cloves, and an herb bunch, and set to cook gently with lid on.

Remarks.—If the vegetables used are old or inferior in quality, they might be put to soak in bicarbonated water; but this only long enough to swell them slightly, about one and one-half hours.

A prolonged soaking of dried vegetables may give rise to incipient germination, and this, by impairing the principles of the vegetables, depreciates the value of the food, and may even cause some harm to the diner.

275—BRAISED VEGETABLES   Légumes Braisés

Vegetables to be *braised* must be first *blanched*, cooled, pared, and tied.

Garnish the bottom of a saucepan with *blanched* pork-rind, sliced carrots and onions, and an herb bunch, and cover the sides of the utensil with thin slices of bacon. Lay the vegetables upon the prepared bed, and leave them to sweat in the oven for about ten minutes with lid on. The object of this oven-sweating is to expel the water. Now moisten enough to cover with white stock (10), and set to cook gently.

This done, drain, remove string, and cut to the shape required. Lay them in a saucepan, and, if they are to be served soon, cover them with their reduced stock from which the grease has been removed.

If they are prepared in advance, simply put them aside in suitable bowls, cover them with their cooking-liquor, which should be strained over them, boiling, and without its grease removed, and cover with waxed paper.

Auxiliary Helps to Braised Vegetables

According to the case, the auxiliary is either the *braising*-liquor, reduced and with all grease removed, or the same completed by means of an addition of meat-*glaze* (15).

Occasionally, it may be the *braising*-liquor slightly thickened with half-*glaze* (23) and finished with butter and the juice of a lemon.

276—BINDING OF GREEN VEGETABLES WITH BUTTER
Liaison des Légumes Verts au Beurre

First thoroughly drain the cooked vegetables and toss them over the fire for a few minutes, in order to completely rid them of their moisture. Season according to the kind of vegetable; add the butter away from the fire, and toss lightly, rolling the saucepan meanwhile on the stove with the view of effecting the blending by means of the mixing of the butter with the treated vegetables.

277—BINDING OF VEGETABLES WITH CREAM
Liaison des Légumes à la Crème

Vegetables to be treated in this way must be kept somewhat firm in cooking. After having thoroughly drained them, put them into a saucepan with enough boiling fresh cream to well moisten without covering them.

Finish their cooking process in the cream, stirring occasionally.

When the cream is almost entirely reduced, finish, away from the fire, with a little butter.

The binding may be slightly stiffened, if necessary, by means of a few tablespoons of cream sauce (79).

278—VEGETABLE CREAMS AND PUREES
Crèmes de Légumes et Purées

Purées of dry and starchy vegetables may be obtained by rubbing the latter through a sieve.

Put the *purée* into a saucepan, and dry it over a brisk fire, adding one and one-half oz. of butter per pint of *purée;* then add milk or cream in small quantities at a time, until the *purée* has reached the required degree of consistency.

For *purées* of succulent vegetables, such as string beans, cauliflowers, celery, etc., a quarter of their volume of mashed potatoes should be added to them in order to effect the binding.

In the case of vegetable creams, substitute for the thickening of mashed potatoes an equivalent quantity of succulent and stiff Béchamel sauce (28).

279—GARNISHES   *Garnitures*

In cookery, although garnishes only play a minor part, they are, nevertheless, very important, for, besides being the principal accompaniments to dishes, they are very often the adornment, while it frequently happens that their harmonious arrangement considerably helps to throw the beauty of a fine joint or bird into relief.

A garnish may consist of one or more products. Be this as it may, its name, as a rule, distinctly denotes, in a word, what it is and how it is made.

In any case, it should always bear some relation to the piece it accompanies, either in the ingredients of its preparation or with regard to the size of the piece constituting the dish.

I merely add that, since the ingredients of garnishes are strictly denoted by the name the latter bear, any addition of products foreign to their nature would be a grave mistake. Likewise, the omission of any parts is to be avoided, as the garnish would thereby be out of keeping with its specified character.

Only in very exceptional circumstances should any change of this kind be allowed to take place.

The ingredients of garnishes are supplied by vegetables, starchy products, *quenelles* of all kinds, cocks' combs and kidneys, truffles and mushrooms, plain or stuffed olives, molluscs (mussels or oysters), shell-fish (crayfish, shrimps, lobster, etc.), butcher's supplies, such as lamb's sweet-bread, calf's brains, and calf's spinal-marrow.

As a rule, garnishes are independent of the dish itself—that is to say, they are prepared entirely apart. At other times they are mixed with it, playing the double part of garnish and condimentary principle, as in the case of *Matelotes, Compotes,* Civets, etc.

Vegetables for garnishing are fashioned and treated in accordance with the use and shape implied by the name of the dish, which should always be the cook's guide in this respect.

The starchy ones, the molluscs and shell-fish, undergo the customary preparation.

I have already described (189 et seq.) the preparation of *quenelles* and *forcemeats* for *garnishing*.

APPENDIX

(Following are the recipes referred to in the main body of this book. The identifying numbers are those originally given to the recipes in the complete American edition of THE ESCOFFIER COOK BOOK.)

281—ANCHOVY BUTTER *Beurre d'Anchois*

Wash twelve or fifteen anchovies in cold water, and dry them thoroughly. Remove the fillets from the bones, pound them smoothly with four oz. of butter, rub through a fine sieve, smooth it with a spoon, and put aside.

856—NORMAN SOLE *Sole Normande*

Poach the sole on a buttered dish with one-sixth pint of fish *fumet,* and the same quantity of the cooking-liquor of mushrooms. Drain, and surround it with mussels, *poached* oysters bearded, shrimps' tails, and small cooked mushrooms. Put the sole in the oven for a few minutes, tilt the dish in order to pour off all liquid, and coat the sole and the garnish with Normande sauce (99). Make a little garland of pale meat-*glaze* (15) on the sauce, and finish the garnish with the following:—Six fine slices of truffle set in a row upon the sole; six small bread crusts in the shape of diamonds, fried in clarified butter (175) and arranged round the truffles; four smelts treated *à l'anglaise* and fried at the last moment; and four medium-sized trussed crayfish cooked in *court-bouillon*.

Set the smelts and the crayfish round the dish.

939—LOBSTER AMERICAN STYLE *Homard à l'Américaine*

The first essential condition is that the lobster should be alive. Sever and slightly crush the claws, with the view of withdrawing their meat after cooking; cut the tail into sections; split the shell in two lengthwise, and remove the queen (a little bag near the head containing some gravel). Put aside, on a plate, the intestines and the coral, which will be used in the finishing of the sauce, and season the pieces of lobster with salt and pepper.

Put these pieces into a saucepan containing one-sixth pint of oil and one oz. of butter, both very hot. Fry them over an open fire until the meat has cooked well and the shell is of a fine red color.

Then remove all fat by tilting the saucepan on its side with its lid on; sprinkle the pieces of lobster with two chopped shallots and one crushed clove of garlic; add one-third pint of white wine, one-quarter pint of fish *fumet*, a small glassful of burnt brandy, one tablespoon of melted meat-*glaze* (15), three small, fresh pressed, and chopped tomatoes (or, failing fresh tomatoes, two tablespoons of tomato *purée*), a pinch of chopped parsley, and a very little cayenne. Cover the saucepan, and set to cook in the oven for eighteen or twenty minutes.

This done, transfer the pieces of lobster to a dish; take out the meat from the section of the tail and the claws, and put them in a *timbale;* set upright the two halves of the shell, and let them lie against each other. Keep the whole hot.

Now reduce the cooking-sauce of the lobster to one-third pint; add the intestines and the chopped coral, together with a piece of butter the size of a walnut; set to cook for a moment, and pass through a strainer.

Put this *cullis* into a pot; heat it without letting it boil, and add, away from the fire, three oz. of butter cut into small pieces.

Pour this sauce over the pieces of lobster which have been kept hot, and sprinkle with a pinch of chopped and scalded parsley.

1037—MATELOTE WITH RED WINE   *Matelote au Vin Rouge*

The fish used for the *Matelote* are eel, carp, tench, bream, perch, etc. It may be prepared from one or many kinds of fish.

Put the fish, cut into sections, into a saucepan. For two lbs. of it, add one minced onion, one herb bunch, two cloves of garlic, one pint of red wine, a pinch of salt, and another of pepper or four peppercorns.

Set to boil; add three tablespoons of heated and burnt brandy; cover the saucepan, and complete the cooking of the fish.

This done, transfer the pieces to another saucepan; strain the cooking-liquor, reduce it by a third, and thicken it with *manié* butter (consisting of one and one-half oz. of butter and two tablespoons of flour), cut into small pieces.

When the binding has been properly done, pour the resulting sauce over the pieces of fish; heat, and serve in a earthenware *timbale*.

1038—MATELOTE WITH WHITE WINE   *Matelote au Vin Blanc*

Prepare the fish as above, but use red wine instead of white, and burn the brandy as before. When the pieces of fish are cooked, transfer them to another saucepan with small onions, previously cooked in butter, and small, cooked mushrooms. Strain the cooking-liquor, reduce it to a little less than half, thicken it with fish velouté (26a), and finish with one oz. of butter.

Pour this sauce over the fish and the garnish; put it in a *timbale* or a deep dish, and surround with crayfish, cooked in *court-bouillon*, and little *croutons* in the shape of hearts, fried in butter.

1076—TENDERLOIN STEAK—*Le Bifteck*; THICK TENDERLOIN— *Châteaubriand*; TOURNEDOS—*Tournedos*; FILET MIGNON— *Filet Mignon*

The French method of cutting meat is not the same as the method used in the United States. Therefore if it is desired to cook the cuts indicated herein, ask your butcher to cut the piece according to the methods described below.

The large beef tenderloin is cut across in different thicknesses. These slices of tenderloin weighing about four and one-half to six pounds have different names according to the section of the tenderloin from which they are cut and according to their thickness.

The "head" end of the tenderloin is cut from the fillet steak called *le bifteck* in France. These steaks are usually not thick, and weigh about five or six ounces.

Next comes the Châuteaubriand, procured from the center of the tenderloin. Its weight is often two or three times that of the ordinary fillet steak. It is cut thick and weighs twelve ounces or more.

Tournedos are the small steaks according to weight. They are cut from the narrower part of the tenderloin, and are cut and trimmed to about two to one slice. They could be called the "kernels" or "noisettes." They should be about one and one-half inches thick, but trimmed round and small. Usually two or three tournedos are served as a portion, weighing about two and one-half ounces each. They are tied together to hold their shape.

The filet mignon comes from the narrowest pointed flat end of the tenderloin of beef and they are cut in various thicknesses according to desire. They also may be tied if necessary.

The fillet steak, as a rule, especially when grilled, constitutes a special meat dish for luncheons; when it is cooked in the saucepan, or *sautéd*, it is more often served as a Relevé.

The same garnishes suit fillet steaks, Châteaubriands, and tournedos, the only necessary modifications being in respect of size and arrangement, which should be subject to the size of the piece of meat.

Whole fillets, fillet steaks, and tournedos may thus be served with garnishes of *braised* celery, tuberous fennel, Swiss chard with gravy, chayote and Belgian endives, *braised* lettuce, various *purées*, etc., and, generally, with all vegetables.

1316a—MUTTON CHOPS REFORME
Côtelettes de Mouton à la Reforme

Trim six mutton chops; season them; dip them in melted butter, and roll them in bread-crumbs, combined with finely-chopped ham in the proportion of a third of the weight of the bread-crumbs. Now cook them gently in clarified butter (175).

Dish them in a circle on a hot dish, and send the following sauce to the table with them:—

Take a small saucepan, and mix three tablespoons of half-*glaze* sauce (23), the same quantity of Poivrade sauce (49), and one teaspoon of red-currant jelly; add one teaspoon of each of the following short *julienne* garnishes to the sauce: hard-boiled white of egg; very red, cured tongue; gherkins; mushrooms, and truffles.

1444—THE WAY TO SERVE POULTRY RELEVES QUICKLY AND HOT
Façon de Servir les Relevés de Volaille Rapidement et Chauds

I feel bound to call the reader's attention to this very important point in culinary work:—

Owing to the difficulties involved in the carving of the fowl and the placing and arranging of the pieces and their garnish upon the diners' plates—both of which operations require dexterity and expertness, which those in charge very often do not possess, or thanks

to the inefficiency of particular installations, or what not, I have
noticed for some considerable time, that the method of serving large
pieces of poultry is, in many cases, very far from being the right one.

For, indeed, how often does not the diner find himself presented
with a plate of fowl which is neither appetizing or sufficiently hot!
It follows from this, that all the care and trouble devoted by a chef
to the preparation of the dish are entirely wasted. Now, I have tried
to improve this state of affairs, by planning a method of serving
which would be at once simple and quick, without necessarily de-
tracting from its tastefulness and presentability.

In the first place, it is my practice to remove the fowl's two
suprêmes, breast fillets, in the kitchen, and to keep them warm in
a little cooking-liquor until the last minute. Secondly, I remove all
the bones of the breast, and I reconstruct the fowl with a stuffing
in keeping with the dish. Either a *mousseline forcemeat*, pilaff rice
combined with cream, *foie gras* and truffles, spaghetti, or noodles
with cream.

Having properly smoothed and arranged the selected stuffing,
the fowl may now be placed, either at one end of a long platter, or
on a low bed of fried bread, on which it may be set firmly.

It may also be entirely coated with Mornay sauce (91), sprinkled
with grated cheese, and speedily *glazed*.

When the bird is ready to serve, its stuffing should be set round it
in fine, *tartlet crusts;* its breasts, quickly sliced, should be distributed
among the *tartlets*, and the platter sent to the table with the sauce
separately.

By this means, it reaches the table hot, it is served quickly and
cleanly; and every person gets a slice of meat, and not the stuffing
only, as was so often the case formerly.

Instead of *tartlets,* one may use thin *croûtons* of bread, of the size
of the slices of chicken, and fried in fresh butter.

To serve, prepare as many *croûtons* and slices of *foie-gras, sautéd*
in butter, as there are diners, and arrange them round the pullet—
the slices of *foie-gras* lying on the *croûtons*. Now, quickly cut the
suprêmes into slices; put one of these on each slice of *foie-gras,* and
on each of the latter put a slice of truffle. Put the pullet, thus prepared, in the oven for a few minutes; let it get very hot, and send it
to the table with the sauce separately.

In the dining-room the Maître-d'hôtel, or at home whoever is waiting on the table, quickly serves the garnished *croûtons* on hot plates, beside each *croûton* he puts a tablespoon of the rice with which the pullet has been stuffed, and, finally, a tablespoon of sauce.

In less than two minutes after its entrance into the dining-room, the pullet is thus served warm to each person.

Of course, the above measures refer to the fowl that has to be served whole; but, when this is not required, the rice removed from the cooked bird need only be set in the center of a deep, square entrée dish (fitted with a cover), and surrounded by the sliced *suprêmes*, with inserted slices of *foie-gras* and truffle. The sauce is also served separately in this case. Cover the dish, so that it may stand and keep hot a few minutes, if necessary, without spoiling.

The legs, which are rarely served at a well-ordered dinner, remain in the kitchen together with the remains.

I cannot too strongly recommend the system just described, whenever the circumstances allow of its being put into practice. It is the only one that ensures an efficient service, calculated to give entire satisfaction to all concerned.

(For convenient carving and serving of poultry or roasts, it is best to have the piece repose on a bed of bread or rice. This will keep any food indicated from slipping on the platter.—Ed.)

1754—ROUENNAIS DUCKLING *Caneton Rouennais*

Except for the one case when they are served cold "à la cuiller," Pekin, Rouen ducklings are not *braised:* they are roasted and always kept underdone. When they have to be stuffed, the *forcemeat* is prepared as follows:—Fry four oz. of larding bacon, cut into dice, with one oz. of chopped onion, and add one-half lb. of sliced ducks' livers, a pinch of chopped parsley, salt, pepper, and a little spice.

Keep the livers underdone, merely browned; let the whole half-cool; grind it, and rub through a fine sieve.

2254—INDIA RICE *Riz à l'Indienne*

Parboil one-half lb. of Patna (Persian) rice in salted water, for fifteen minutes; stirring it from time to time the while.

Drain it; wash it in several cold waters; lay it on a napkin, and set the latter on a tray or on a sieve. Dry for fifteen minutes in a steamer or in a very moderate oven.

2344—THE COOKING OF SUGAR   *Le Cuisson du Sucre*

From the state of syrup to the most highly-concentrated state in which it is used in pastry, sugar passes through various stages of cooking, which are:—The small thread (215° F.) and the large thread (222° F.), the small ball (236° F.) and the large ball (248° F.), the small crack (285° F.) and the large crack (315° F.). When the last state is overreached, the sugar has become caramel (360° F.).

Put the necessary quantity of sugar in a small, copper or stainless steel pot; moisten with enough water to melt it, and boil. Carefully remove the scum which forms, and which might cause the sugar to granulate.

As soon as the sugar begins to move stiffly in boiling, it is a sign that the water has almost entirely evaporated, and that the real cooking of the sugar has begun.

From this moment, with moistened fingers or a little piece of moistened linen, take care to remove the crystallized sugar from the sides of the utensil, lest it make the remaining portion turn.

The cooking of the sugar then progresses very rapidly, and the states of its various stages, coming one upon the other in quick succession at intervals of a few minutes, may be ascertained as follows:—

It has reached the *small-thread stage,* when a drop of it held between the thumb and the first finger forms small resistless strings when the thumb and finger are drawn apart.

It has reached the *large-thread stage,* when, proceeding in the same way, the strings formed between the parted finger and thumb are more numerous and stronger.

From this moment care must be taken to use cold water in order to ascertain the state of the sugar.

When a few minutes have elapsed after the test for the large-thread state, dip the end of the first finger, first into cold water, then into the sugar, and plunge it again immediately into the bowl of cold water, which should be at hand. The sugar taken from the finger forms a kind of soft ball, and it is this state which is called the *small ball.*

When, upon repeating the procedure, the sugar removed from the finger rolls into a firmer ball, the *large-ball stage* is reached.

After the cooking has continued for a few seconds longer, the sugar lying on the finger peels off in the form of a thin, flexible film, which sticks to the teeth. This is the *small-crack stage*. Tests should then be made in quick succession, until the film taken from the end of the finger breaks "clean" in the teeth, like glass. This is the *large-crack state,* the last of the cooking stages, and as soon as it has been reached the utensil should be taken off the fire, lest a few seconds more turn the sugar to *caramel.*

To prevent the granulating of the sugar, a few drops of lemon juice may be added to it; or, better still, a tablespoon of glucose per lb.

2354—ESSENCES AND FLAVORINGS   *Essences et Assaisonements*

The various *essences* used in pastry are bought ready-made. The flavorings consist of those products treated by infusion, such as vanilla; of grated or infused products, such as lemon and orange peels; and liqueurs in general.

Fruit juices only become flavors when a liqueur in keeping with the fruit from which they were extracted has been added to them.

2374—COMMON CREAM PUFF PASTE (FOR SOUFFLE FRITTERS, GNOCHI, POTATOES A LA DAUPHINE)   *Pâte à Chou Commune*

Proceed as directed above, but reduce the quantity of butter to three oz., and the number of eggs to twelve; avoid drying this paste too much.

INDEX

144